SEMIOTEXT(E) FOREIGN AGENTS SERIES

Published by Semiotext(e)
2007 Wilshire Blvd., Suite 427, Los Angeles, CA 90057
www.semiotexte.com

Special thanks to Lionel Casson, Glen Milstein, Brett Phares, and Robert
Dewhurst for copy editing; and to Federico Boccaccini for research assistance.

Cover and inside Art by Michal Rovner.
Cover: *Flower*, 2004, steel table, one Petri dish and digital projection.
First page: *Untitled (Spiral Lines)*.
Copyright: Michal Rovner/ Artists Rights Society (ARS), New York.
Courtesy: PaceWildenstein Gallery

Design by Hedi El Kholti
ISBN: 978-1-58435-050-7
Distributed by The MIT Press, Cambridge, Mass. and London, England

MULTITUDE

BETWEEN INNOVATION
AND NEGATION

Paolo Virno

Translated by Isabella Bertoletti, James Cascaito,
and Andrea Casson

\<e\>

*To Luciano Ferrari Bravo, who, perhaps,
would have laughed at all of this.*

Contents

PART 1

SO-CALLED "EVIL" AND

CRITICISM OF THE STATE

The Animal Open to the World

There is no objective investigation of human nature that does not carry with it, like a clandestine traveler, at least the trace of a theory of political institutions. The sifting of species-specific instincts and drives, the analysis of a mind amply distinguished by linguistic ability, the recognition of the thorny relationship between individual human animals and their kin: this process always conceals a judgment on the legitimacy of the Minister of the Interior. And vice versa: there is no theory of political institutions worthy of its name that does not assume, as its ill-concealed supposition, one or the other of the representations of the traits that distinguish *Homo sapiens* from other animal species. To limit ourselves to a high school example, little is understood of Hobbes's *Leviathan* if one neglects his *De Homine*.

Let us avoid any misunderstandings: it would be unrealistic, indeed farcical, to believe that a model of a just society can be deduced from certain bioanthropological constants. Every political program takes root in a historicosocial context without precedents (the civil wars of religion, in the case of Hobbes, a productive process based directly upon the power of verbal thought, in our case); each political program measures itself by means of a not-yet public constellation of passions and interests. However, collective action is truly contingent *precisely because*, while it tightens its hold on the most fleeting actuality, it also burdens itself in changing, unexpected ways with that which is not contingent, that is to say, with bioanthropological constants. The particular and unrepeatable character of a political decision, the obligation to act in due course, the perception that yesterday would have been too early and tomorrow will be too late: these are not dissolved by the reference to human nature; they are, instead, accentuated to the highest degree.

The connection between anthropological reflection and theory of institutions was formulated, in quite an unreserved manner, by Carl Schmitt, in the seventh chapter of his *The Concept of the Political*:

> One could test all theories of state and political ideas according to their anthropology and thereby classify these as to whether they consciously or unconsciously presuppose man to be by nature evil or by nature good. The distinction is to be taken here in a rather summary fashion and not in any specifically moral or ethical sense. The problematic or unproblematic conception of man is decisive for the presupposition of every further political consideration, the answer to the question whether man is a dangerous being or not, a risky or a harmless creature. [...]
>
> Helmuth Plessner, who as the first modern philosopher in his book *Macht und menschliche Natur* dared to advance a political anthropology of a grand style, correctly says that there exists no philosophy and no anthropology which is not politically relevant [...] He has recognized in particular that philosophy and anthropology, as specifically applicable to the totality of knowledge, cannot, like any specialized discipline, be neutralized against irrational life decisions. Man, for

Plessner, is "primarily a being capable of creating distance" who in his essence is undetermined, unfathomable, and remains an "open question." If one bears in mind the anthropological distinction of evil and good and combines Plessner's "remaining open" with his positive reference to danger, Plessner's theory is closer to evil than to goodness. [...]

I have pointed out several times that the antagonism between the so-called authoritarian and anarchist theories can be traced to these formulas. [...] Ingenuous anarchism reveals that the belief in the natural goodness of man is closely tied to the radical denial of state and government. One follows from the other, and both foment each other. [...] The radicalism vis-à-vis state and government grows in proportion to the radical belief in the goodness of man's nature. [...] What remains is the remarkable and, for many, certainly disquieting diagnosis that all genuine political theories presuppose man to be evil, i.e., by no means an unproblematic but a dangerous and dynamic being. (Schmitt, *Concept*: 58–61)

If man were a meek animal, dedicated to mutual understanding and reciprocal recognition, there would be no need whatsoever for disciplinary and coercive institutions. The criticism of the State, developed with various intensity by liberals, anarchists, and communists, is nourished, according to Schmitt, by the prejudicial idea of a "natural goodness" in our species. An authoritative example of this tendency is established, today, by the libertarian political positions of Noam Chomsky. He supports, with admirable tenacity, the dissolution of the central apparatus of power, accusing this apparatus of humiliating the inborn creativity of verbal language, that is, the species-specific requirement capable of guaranteeing to the human community a self-government free of consolidated hierarchies. If, however, as everything leads us to believe, *Homo sapiens* is a dangerous, unstable and (self)destructive animal, then in order to hold this animal in check, the formation of a "united political body" seems inevitable; a political body that would exercise, in the words of Schmitt, an unconditional "monopoly of political decision." This diagnosis cannot be ascribed solely to the authoritarian inclinations of the author alone, as is demonstrated by the fact that it coincides, essentially, with that of the illuminist Freud:

> [Institutional] order is a kind of compulsion to repeat which, when a regulation has been laid down once and for all, decides when, where and how a thing shall be done, so that in every similar circumstance one is spared hesitation and indecision (Freud, *Civilization*: 46).

> The element of truth behind all this [behind the impossibility of loving one's neighbour according to Christian law (my explanation)], which people are so ready to disavow, is that men are not gentle creatures who want to be loved, and who at the most can defend themselves if they are attacked; they are, on the contrary, creatures among whose instinctual endowments is to be reckoned a powerful share of aggressiveness. As a result, their neighbour is for them not only a potential helper or sexual object, but also someone who tempts them to satisfy their aggressiveness on him, to exploit his capacity for work without compensation, to use him sexually without his consent, to seize his possessions, to humiliate him, to cause him pain, to torture and to kill him. *Homo homini lupus*: who [...] has the courage to dispute this assertion? As a rule this cruel aggressiveness waits for some provocation or puts itself at the service of some

other purpose, whose goal might also have been reached by milder measures. In circumstances that are favorable to it, when the mental counter-forces which ordinarily inhibit it are out of action, it also manifests itself spontaneously and reveals man as a savage beast to whom consideration towards his own kind is something alien (ibid: 68–69).

The communists believe that they have found the path to deliverance from our evils. According to them, man is wholly good and well-disposed to his neighbor; but the institution of private property has corrupted his nature. [...] If private property were abolished, all wealth held in common, and everyone allowed to share in the enjoyment of it, ill-will and hostility would disappear among men. [...] I have no concern with any economic criticisms of the communist system;[...], but I am able to recognize that the psychological premises on which the system is based are an untenable illusion. In abolishing private property we deprive the human love of aggression of one of its instruments, certainly a strong one, though certainly not the strongest; but we have in no way altered the differences in power and influence which are misused by aggressiveness, nor have we altered anything in its nature (ibid: 70–71).

It is not wise to turn up one's philosophically sophisticated little nose in the face of the crude choice between: "man is by nature good," and "man is by nature bad." This is not wise because, in the first place, Schmitt himself is well aware of such crudeness: he uses this stenographic simplification on purpose to evoke a bioanthropological background that, having nothing to do with naïve moral qualifications, provokes, instead, quite a few theoretical brain teasers. But it is also not wise to turn up one's nose, above all, for another reason. It is exactly this apparent coarseness, in fact, that helps us to enunciate in a straightforward manner the historiconaturalistic hypothesis that, by disrupting the conceptual scheme delineated by Schmitt, results in being something truly interesting. Here it is: the risky instability of the human animal—so-called *evil*, in sum—does not imply at all the formation and maintenance of that "supreme empire" that is the sovereignty of the State. On the contrary, "hostile radicalism towards the State" and towards the capitalist means of production, far from taking for granted the innate meekness of our species, can construct its own authentic pedestal in full recognition of the "problematic" temperament of the human animal, which is undefined and potential, (thus, also dangerous). The criticism of the "monopoly of political decision making" and, in general, of institutions whose rules function as a form of repeated coercion, must stand firmly upon the determination that man is "evil by nature."

1. Driven Excess and Modality of the Possible

What is this "evil" made up of, this "evil" with which, in the words of Schmitt, every theory of institutions that demonstrates an ounce of realism with regard to human nature never ceases to create a confrontation? He refers, even if fleetingly, to the theses of the most democratic among the founding members of philosophical anthropology, Helmuth Plessner. Here, however, I limit myself to calling up a few of the fundamental notions of philosophical anthropology considered in its entirety, omitting any distinction (relevant in other contexts) among individual authors.

Man is "problematic," according to Plessner, and also according to Gehlen, because he is devoid of a defined environment, thus corresponding, point by point, to his psychosomatic configuration and to his aggressive drive. If an animal trapped in an environment reacts with innate self-certainty to external stimuli, translating them into a repertory of behaviors that serve to protect it, man, disoriented as he is, has to confront a profusion of urges lacking any precise biological aims. Our species is distinguished by its "openness to the world"—"world" meaning a vital context that always remains partially undetermined and unpredictable. The overabundance of stimuli that are not connected to one operating task or another provokes a constant uncertainty and a disorientation that can never be fully reversed. In Plessner's terms, the animal "open to the world" always maintains a disconnection, a "separation," with regard to the states of things and to the events it runs up against. The opening to the world, with the very high level of undifferentiated potentiality involved, is correlated in a philogenetic profile, to sparse instinctual specialization, not only with regard to the newly born, but also with regard to the permanence of infantile characteristics found also in adult subjects.

These somewhat stereotypical signals, however, are sufficient for describing in detail the "dangerousness" of *Homo sapiens*, upon which, according to Schmitt, the modern theory of sovereignty of the State rests its case (and which, according to Freud, can be mitigated solely by a normative ordinance totally equivalent to the compulsion to repeat). The overabundance of stimuli not yet finalized biologically and the resulting variability of behaviors go hand in hand with a congenital fragility of inhibitive mechanisms. The animal "open to the world" gives proof of a virtually unlimited species-specific aggressiveness, whose unleashed causes can never be reduced to a defined catalogue (habitable density of a territory, sexual selection, etc.), since these causes are also variable to the point of being immeasurable (see Lorenz, *On Aggression*). Struggles for sheer prestige, and even the notion of "honor" itself, have a very close connection to the drive-induced structure of a living being who is disoriented and, for this very reason, is in a state of potentiality. The lack of an unambiguous *habitat* is such that man is a "cultural being by nature" (Gehlen, *Man*: 108). However, it is precisely culture, as an innate biological device, that exhibits substantial ambivalence: it smoothes out danger; but in other instances, it multiplies and diversifies the occasions of risk: "it defends man from his own nature," keeping him from experiencing his "own terrifying plasticity and indecision" (Gehlen, *L'Origine*: 97). And yet, since it is itself the very manifestation of this plasticity and indecision, culture favors at one and the same time the full deployment of that nature against which it should offer defense.

So-called "evil" can also be described by redirecting our attention to some salient prerogatives of verbal language. Problematic, or, better yet, unstable and dangerous, is the animal whose life is characterized by *negation*, by the *modality of the possible*, by *regression to the infinite*. It goes without saying that these three linguistic structures constitute the logical base of the entire metaphysical tradition. And that each of them refers to the other two: negation highlights that which, even if being actually false or non-existent, is nonetheless considered possible. Furthermore, since it works upon a preliminary affirmative assertion, the "not" is the original manifestation of that discourse-upon-discourse that triggers the regression of meta-languages to the infinite. What is most important, however, is that these three structures summarize the emotional situation of a disoriented animal. Negation is equivalent to a certain degree of "separation" from its own vital context, sometimes, in fact, with a provisional delay of a sensory stimulus. The modality of the possible coincides with driven excesses, not yet, biologically finalized, and also with the unspecialized character of the human animal. The regression toward the infinite expresses the "opening to the world" as a chronic form of incompleteness, or also—but this is the same thing—as a vain search for that proportionality between drives and behaviors that is, instead, the prerogative of a circumscribed environment. The logical base of metaphysics offers, simultaneously, the plot of a theory of passions. Sorrow, sympathy, desire, fear, aggression: these affects, that we share with many other animal species, are reshaped from top to bottom by negation, by the modality of the possible, by the regression toward the infinite. There are also affects that, far from being re-shaped, are indeed provoked by these linguistic structures: *boredom*, for example, is none other than the emotional equivalent of the regression toward the infinite, of the petrified movement that seems at one moment to remove a limit, only in order to then reestablish it, again and again. Similarly, *anguish*, (that is, an indeterminate fear, not linked to one or another state of affairs) is the sentimental flap of the condition of the possible. With regard to negation, it is precisely to this negation that we owe the eventual *failure of reciprocal recognition* between members of the same species (see the closing essay of this book, "Mirror Neurons, Linguistic Negation, Reciprocal Recognition"). The perceptive evidence that "this is a man" loses its own indisputability once it is subject to the functioning of the "not": cannibalism and Auschwitz are proof of this. Located at the limit of social interaction, the eventuality of nonrecognition reverberates, even at its center, and permeates the entire web. Language, far from mitigating intra-species aggression (as Habermas and a certain number of happy-go-lucky philosophers assure us), radicalizes this aggression beyond measure.

2. Ambivalence

The dangerousness of our species is as extensive as its capacity to execute innovative actions; that is to say, innovative actions capable of modifying customs and consolidated norms. Whether one speaks of excessive drive, or of linguistic negation, of a "separation" from one's own vital context, or of the modality of the possible, it is abundantly evident that we are speaking, only in one fell swoop, of the premises of the abuse of power and of torture. We speak in a similar manner of the requirements that allow for the invention of works councils or of other democratic organisms based on that typically political passion that is *friendship without familiarity*. Both "virtue" and "evil" require a deficit of instinctual orientation, and they feed off the uncertainty experienced in the face of "that which can be different from the way it is"; this is how Aristotle (*Ethics*) defines the contingency that distinguishes the praxis of the "animal in possession of language." The biolinguistic conditions of so-called "evil" are the same biolinguistic conditions that animate "virtue." Suffice it to reconsider negation: negation is capable of tearing away, or of placing between parentheses, the empathy between members of the same species that is guaranteed by the cerebral device of mirror neurons, allowing us to enunciate something like "this is *not* a man" in the presence of a Jew or an Arab [Translators' note: see the closing essay of this book]. One must add, however, that the eventuality of reciprocal *not*-recognizing reality is kept at bay (virtuously, of course) by the same faculty that allows us to negate any semantic content that has rendered this faculty possible. The public sphere—interwoven with persuasive discourses, political conflicts, pacts, and collective projects—is none other than a second negation by means of which one represses anew the first negation, that is, the syntagm "non-man."

The public sphere consists, in short, of a *negation of the negation*: "non non-man." The obvious identity between the species-specific resources of which virtuous innovation avails itself and those resources from which homicidal hostility is drawn, does not authorize us, not even for a moment, however, to sweeten the "evil," by considering it to be limited, a mishap, or worse, the indispensable propelling agent of the "good." On the contrary: truly *radical* evil, irrepressible and lacerating, is precisely and solely the evil that shares the same root as the good life.

The full coextensiveness between danger and protection from danger allows us to place the problem of political institutions upon more solid bases. There are at least two reasons for this. First of all, because this coextensiveness causes us to doubt that apparent protection (sovereignty of the State, for example) might constitute, in certain cases, the most intense manifestation of danger (intraspecies aggression). Next, because it suggests a methodological criterion of some importance: institutions actually protect us if, and only if, they avail themselves of the same underlying conditions that, in other ways, never cease to stir up a threat. Institutions protect us, if, and only if, they derive apotropaic resources from the "opening to the world" and from the ability to negate, from the neotenic condition and from the modality of the possible. They protect us, if, and only if, they exhibit at all times that they belong to the sphere of "that which can be different from the way it is."

Contemporary critical thought—from Chomsky to French poststructuralism—has attempted to overcome the dialectical schema according to which the (self)destructive drives of the linguistic animal would be destined to strengthen and perfect, again and again, the synthesis of the State. This "school" of thought has found it convenient to expunge from its own horizon, together with the dialectic, even the very memory of those (self)destructive drives. In this way, contemporary critical thought runs the risk of corroborating Schmitt's diagnosis: radicalism hostile toward the State grows in equal measure with faith in the radical good of human nature. We are evidently dealing here with a dead end. Rather than repealing the negative, even in order to escape from the dialectical millstone, it is necessary to develop a nondialectical understanding of the negative. Three key-words are useful here: ambivalence, oscillation, perturbing. *Ambivalence*: this friendship without familiarity, the authentic fulcrum of a political community, can always capsize into a familiarity loaded with enmity that instigates massacres between factions, gangs, tribes. There is no resolving third term, no dialectical synthesis, no superior point of equilibrium: each polarity refers to the other; indeed, each already contains the other in itself, already allows a glimpse of it inside its own intricate structure. *Oscillation*: the reciprocal recognition between members of the same species, marked by an incessant pendular movement that swings from partial success to incipient failure. *Perturbing*: frightening is never the unusual state of things; frightening is merely that state with which we are most familiar (excessive drive, fundamental structures of verbal language), which, under different circumstances, has also assumed, or can assume, a protective function.

3. Murmurings in the Desert

The relationship between the dreadful aspects of human nature and political institutions is, without a doubt, a metahistorical question. In order to confront this relationship, it serves little purpose to recall the kaleidoscope of cultural differences. However, as always happens, a metahistorical question gains visibility and significance only in a concrete historicosocial junction. The unchangeable, that is, the congenital (self)destructiveness of the animal that thinks with words, is brought to the table as an "argument" of a "function" created entirely by crises and contingent conflicts. To put it in other words: the problem of aggression within the same species will come to center stage *when* the modern central State experiences a huge decline, studded, however, with convulsive restorative thrusts and with disturbing metamorphoses. It is both within the course of this decline, and on account of it, that the problem of institutions, that is, of their role as stabilizers and regulators, returns to assert itself in all its bioanthropological capacity.

It is Schmitt again who ascertains with evident bitterness the collapse of the sovereignty of the state: "The epoch of Statehood is already reaching an end [...]. The state as model of political unity, the state as holder of the most extraordinary of all monopolies, that is, of the monopoly of political decision, is about to be dethroned" (Schmitt, *Concept*: from his introduction to the 1963 edition of *Der Begriff des Politischen*; published in Italian in *Le Categorie del "politico": Saggi di teoria politica* [Bologna: Mulino, 1972]; English rendering by the translators). The crumbling of the "monopoly of political decision" derives as much from the nature of the relevant productive process (based on abstract knowledge and linguistic communication) as it does from the social uprisings of the 1960s and 1970s, and from the subsequent proliferation of forms of life resistant to a "preliminary pact of obedience." It is not necessary, here, to linger on these causes or to air other eventual causes. What really counts are the questions that stand out in the new situation. Which political institutions lie outside the apparatus of the State? How to restrain the instability and the dangerousness of the human animal, in circumstances where one can no longer count upon a "coercion to repeat" within the application of rules that are in force from time to time? In what way can excessive drive and the opening to the world serve as a *political* antidote to the poisons that they themselves secrete?

These questions take us back to the harshest episode of the Jewish exodus: the "murmurings" in the desert; that is to say, a sequence of internal conflicts of rare bitterness. Instead of submitting to Pharaoh, or rising up against his rule, the Jews fully utilized the principle of the *tertium datur*, seizing upon an ulterior and previously unacknowledged possibility: abandoning the "house of slavery and iniquitous labor." Thus they move forward into a no-man's land and there they experience not-yet-public forms of self-government. But the bond of solidarity weakens: nostalgia for the ancient oppression grows, respect for their fellow escapees suddenly changes into hatred, and violence and idolatry overflow. Divisions, abuses of power, calumnies, diverse forms of aggression: thus one can see, at the foot of Mount Sinai, "[Man] 'primarily a being capable of creating distance' (Schmitt quotes Plessner here), who in his essence is undetermined, unfathomable, and remains an 'open question'" (Schmitt, *Concept*: 60). The narration of the exodus constitutes, perhaps, the most authoritative theologicopolitical model of going beyond the State. This is because it proposes the possibility of undermining Pharaoh's monopoly of decision making by means of an enterprising withdrawal; but also because, by giving great emphasis to the "murmurings," it excludes the possibility that this withdrawal has at its own foundation the natural meekness of the human animal. The exodus belies Schmitt: a Republic that no longer pertains to the State maintains a rather close relationship, free of illusions, with the innate destructiveness of our species.

2

State of Nature and Civil State

Why is it necessary to obey? This is the only query that counts in a theory of institutions. Whoever would answer: because the law commands it, would be condemned to a regression to infinity. Indeed it is all too easy to ask him, in return: Fine, but why is it necessary to obey a law that imposes obedience? Perhaps one does so in compliance with yet another law, previous or more fundamental? But it is obvious, even with regard to the previous question, that the initial question still stands. Thus, climbing step by step, one never arrives at an end result. It is Hobbes who interrupts this regression to infinity. For him, obedience to laws is justified by a *fact*, in and of itself incommensurate to any normative regulation whatsoever: the passage from the "state of nature" to the "civil state."

This pair of concepts deserves renewed attention. It highlights the link between the dangerousness of *Homo sapiens* and political institutions, unraveling this link in a rather peculiar way. The state of nature is the sphere in which there predominates an overabundance of stimuli that cannot be translated into unequivocal behavior: neoteny, the opening to the world, the lack of congenital inhibitions. Moving away from the state of nature brings with it, on one hand, the possibility for stabilizing the disoriented animal;

on the other hand, it brings the extrajuristic obligation to apply the norms in force in the civil state, with the resulting compulsion to repeat. The necessity to appease fear of a violent death sets up the "monopoly of the political decision." This point is as well known as a proverb. Yet, we must still ask ourselves: what is, when push comes to shove, the effective relationship between the state of nature and the civil state? Is it that between the one and the other there is a true caesura? Or are we facing Siamese twins obliged to take turns to support one another? Are we dealing with polar concepts, or, vice versa, with synonymous terms, terms that share a unique and identical referent? I have already said repeatedly that libertarian political theories do not distinguish themselves from authoritarian political theories because they do not acknowledge the risky "problematic nature" of the human animal. On the contrary: they distinguish themselves from such a situation because they give so much weight to this "density of problems," such as to judge as being minimally plausible (in other words, infinitely risky) every attempt to confine the "density of problems" to a well defined area. To put it in Hobbesian jargon: criticism of sovereignty bases itself, today, on the manifest *impossibility of exiting from the state of nature*. But more about this topic, later.

1. Hobbes's Paradox

Let us observe more closely the way in which the relationship between natural prejuristic life and the public sphere of the State is articulated according to Hobbes. This articulation is resolved by means of an authentic paradox. According to Hobbes, the institution of the "body politic" obliges us to obey, even *before* knowing what will be required of us: "For since our obligation to civil obedience, by virtue whereof the civil laws are valid, is before all civil law." (Hobbes, *Citizen*: 170). For this reason, one will not find a particular law that explicitly commands us not to rebel. If unconditional acceptance of a command had not already been *assumed*, the concrete legislative dispositions (including, obviously, the one that says "you will not rebel") would have no validity whatsoever. Hobbes maintains that the original binding force of obedience is derived from "natural law," that is, from the common interest in self-preservation and in security. However, one is quick to add that "natural law," the Super-law that commands us to obey all the orders of the sovereign, becomes effectively a law only when we have exited from the state of nature, thus, when the state has already been instituted. Here is the paradox in Hobbes: the obligation to obey is, at one and the same time, both the cause and effect of the existence of the State; it is supported by that which is also its own foundation; it precedes and follows, at the same time, the formation of the "supreme empire."

This paradox demonstrates in the most clear fashion how there is both a symbiotic bond, as well as a drastic opposition, between natural life and "unified body politic." The state of nature does not at all coincide with a set of prelinguistic drives; therefore it coincides neither with the search for pleasure nor with the escape from pain. It involves, rather, a way of being in which all the typical human faculties play a role: the alternative between pleasure/pain, that, in and of itself, determines the behavior also of those animals unable to speak. And yet it is integrated (and reformed from top to bottom) by the two dyads useful/harmful and just/unjust, both completely inconceivable outside the realm of verbal thought (See Aristotle, *Politics*). Hobbes observes on more than one occasion how the dangers present in the state of nature do not come from the absence of the *logos*; on the contrary, they derive from its peculiar form of performance. Nonhuman animals, "though they have some use of voice, in making known to one another their desires, and other affections; yet they want that art of words, by which some men can represent to others, that which is good, in the likeness of evil; and evil, in the likeness of good, [...] troubling their peace at their pleasure" (Hobbes, *Leviathan*: 111). Beyond being a source of dissension and an instrument of aggression ("But the tongue of man is a trumpet of war and sedition." [Hobbes, *Citizen*: 66]), verbal language is also, nevertheless, the matrix of shared rules. For this reason, and for this reason only, can we speak, even if it be metaphorically, of a "natural law" directed towards containing the universal inclination to harm one's fellow species. Respect for agreements, fidelity to oaths, equable punishment for wrongdoings, reciprocity of rights: these and other actions are the ways in which the dyad just/unjust is delineated before—a logical "before," obviously—real and actual political institutions arise. Nonetheless, as we know, for Hobbes "natural law" is not an authentic law. It is not authentic, because nothing can guarantee its *application*. One cannot speak of rules (nor, on the other hand, of what is just and unjust); what is lacking is a coercive force that would compel the carrying out of these rules in all particular cases. The civil state breaks its bond with the natural state because it assures that any norm whatsoever can always be realized, independent from its specific content. "Natural law," which generates the obligation to obey, that is to say, the unconditional application of the rules, becomes an effective *law* only retrospectively, thanks, that is, to the complete affirmation ... of the obligation to obey. Of this natural law one could say: it is the child of its own child.

The state of nature, although totally endowed of linguistic capability, is reduced, nevertheless, to a theater of undifferentiated and polymorphous drives: the rules that lack a particular application, for Hobbes, are not distinguished from the dangerous instability of desires, in as much as they leave the field open for rivalry, for diffidence, for pride. In an equal and opposite manner, the civil state, while still maintaining the excessive drive of the neotenic animal, seems instead to be molded in every detail by verbal thought: the systematic application of the rules silences, according to Hobbes, intraspecies aggression and dissolves every perturbing ambivalence. The natural state shows us the "opening to the world," a world stripped, however, of any criterion of orientation. For its part, the civil state offers a protective orientation, but it places in parentheses that "opening," thus carving out a *pseudoenvironment* in which unequivocal and repetitive behaviors prevail. Both the natural state and the civil state are in possession of an articulation between drives and language at their very center. But in both states, this articulation takes on a form such as to allow only one term at a time to emerge into full view, leaving the other term implicit or irrelevant. In the natural state we have the (drives-)language junction; in the civil state, what prevails instead is the drives (-language) junction. In both cases, the linking hyphen remains hidden. It is such that the articulation between drives and language undergoes, on account of its own pervasiveness, a double and simultaneous discrimination: it no longer seems to be something characteristically *natural*; but it also does not seem to be something characteristically *political*.

In an article in 1939, entitled *Signe zéro*, Roman Jakobson observes that in every dyad of contrasting terms there is a formal asymmetry in force, to which there corresponds, moreover, a semantic asymmetry. Consider, for example, the dyads: lion/lioness, 5/-5, tall/short. The signs "lion", "5," and "tall", says Jakobson, are *unmarked* signs, since they express a category in all its breadth: the entire animal species, not only the male; the number 5, as such, positive or negative as it may be; the vertical extension, whether large or small. Vice versa, "lioness," "-5," and "short" are *marked* signs, given that they isolate a particular property: sexual identity, a precise algebraic condition, a limit of stature. If one examines the dyad natural state/civil state in the light of the distinction proposed by Jakobson, a singular fact is salient: both terms are *marked*. And the marking of each term is perfectly mirrored in the marking of the other term: "natural state" = drives (-language); "civil state"= (drives-) language. The two verbal syntagms, instead of being opposites, are actually synonymous, each syntagm being in possession of the drives-language dyad as its linguistic referent. For this junction to occur, however, there exists no *unmarked* sign, no *signe zéro* that might give an account, in a neutral manner, that is to say, truly comprehensive manner, of its salient characteristics (beginning, as is obvious, with the hyphen). One could object that the modern theory of sovereignty has access to at least one concept capable of functioning as an unmarked sign: the concept of "natural law." But this is an optical illusion. The concept in question is actually subjected to two markings, antithetical and yet simultaneous: "natural law," if it is *natural*, is not (yet) a law; if it is a *law*, it is (no longer) natural. The double marking lies at the origin of Hobbes's paradox, according to which, as we have seen, "natural law" seems to be, at one and the same time, the premise and the consequence of the civil state.

The natural state comes back to assert itself at the center of the "body politic" on two fundamental occasions: a) when the people disintegrate into *multitude*, or into a plurality of individuals who resist the preliminary bond of obedience; b) when the sovereign suspends the ordinary laws and declares a *state of exception*. Let us look at this more clearly. According to Hobbes, the concept of a people is strictly correlated with the existence of the State, indeed it is an echo of the State: "The people is somewhat that is *one*, having one will .... The people rules in all governments" (Hobbes, *Citizen*: 135), and, reciprocally, "the King is the people" (ibid: 135). The multitude, by not transferring its own rights to the sovereign, escapes from the political unit. The multitude is anti-state, but, exactly for this reason, it is also antipeople. "The people stirring up the citizens against the city, that is to say, the multitude against the people" (ibid: 135). A rebellion of this nature comes together in a unity of centrifugal institutions, or "irregular systems" (Hobbes, *Leviathan*: 154) which Hobbes describes, with absolute contempt: "...in their nature but leagues, or sometimes mere concourse of people, without union to any particular design, not by obligation of one to another" (ibid: 154). The insurgence of the multitude finds its overturned equivalent in the state of exception. By promulgating this equivalent, the sovereign himself allows neotenic uncertainty to erupt within the sphere of the "supreme empire." Every question of rights ends up to be, for a moment, a question of facts. The distinction between the *grammatical* plane (the rules of a community) and the *empirical* plane (the facts of life to which those rules should apply) becomes blurred. One could also say: the state of exception, by subverting the pseudo-environmental uniformity assured by civil laws, restores the "opening to the world" to its imponderable circumstances. But it restores this opening, let us note, as an exclusive requisite of sovereignty. Multitude and state of exception: these two categories evoke, even if in an oblique and interstitial manner, that unmarked sign on the basis of which the point of drives-language would be considered as something truly *natural* and, at the same time, something truly *political*.

2. Rules and Regularity

I would like to sketch out here, in order to continue, a succinct interpretation of the dichotomy of the dyad natural state/civil state. Better yet, I would like to translate the problems with which this dichotomy overburdens itself within a different conceptual image, one that is no longer a dichotomy. We know that, for Hobbes, the natural state is lacking in true and real rules because there is no guarantee for the application of these rules. The civil state, by virtue of the preliminary pact of obedience, constitutes instead, an environment in which the application is assured in an almost automatic fashion. On one hand, (psuedo)rules without application; on the other, an application independent of the dictated rules in force from time to time. Such polarization betrays—in the two-fold sense of the word: allowing to leak out, and, at the same time distorting—an otherwise complex biolinguistic question: what does it mean, for the human animal, "to follow a rule?" The observations which Wittgenstein dedicated to this theme offer important cues, in my opinion, for disproving the theoretical paradigm of state sovereignty. Furthermore, these observations allow us to outline in a different manner the relationship between the dangerousness of *Homo sapiens* and political institutions. It is not possible, at least not here, to offer a detailed reconstruction of Wittgenstein's reasoning (see Part Two of my *Jokes and Innovative Action: For a Logic of Change,* which follows this essay). A few brief remarks will have to do, in order to undo Hobbes's paradox.

Rules do not give instructions on how they should be applied in a particular case. Between the norm and its concrete realization there exists a lasting hiatus, a real and true incommensurability. In principle, the same normative content, can lead to possible actions that are diverse, and indeed at times, opposite. Wittgenstein shows how inconclusive is the claim of being able to devise "a rule determining the application of a rule" (Wittgenstein, *Investigations*: 34). It is obvious that this second rule, needing to be applied in its own turn, will require a third (one that can indicate how to apply the rule that governs…the application of the rules); and so it continues, with no outcome. This is not so different, as we shall see, from the regression to the infinite, into which fall, according to Hobbes, those who long to establish upon a law the obligation to obey the laws. To avoid this regression, Hobbes bases the obligation of obedience upon the exit from the natural state and upon the formation of a "joint political body." Wittgenstein's solution is completely different. After having established that the uniform application of the rules depends for the most part on "habits (customs, institutions)," he examines, instead, a critical situation, one in which habits crumble and institutions are no longer up to the task of orienting praxis: "But what if one person reacts in one way and another in another to the order and the training? Which one is right?" (ibid: 70). According to Witttgenstein, it is precisely and only in a situation of this kind that the actual conspiracy of "following a rule" comes to light.

When the application of a norm ends up being uncertain or controversial, it is necessary to return for a moment *to this side of* the norm, adopting as a reference system "the common behavior of mankind," that is to say, a set of practices so basic as to characterize life itself for our species. On this side of the *rules*, says Wittgenstein, there exists a preliminary *regularity*. This term refers to the anthropological background of any positive right. In question are the fundamental aptitudes (that is, the unvarying ones) of the linguistic animal: questioning, responding, negating, elaborating hypotheses, thanking, hating, praying, nurturing hopes and fears, etc. One could even say that the concept of *regularity* indicates the threshold at which language grafts itself repeatedly onto prelinguistic drives and reorganizes them profoundly. The appeal to "the common behavior of mankind" disengages the regression to the infinite that is embedded in the search for "a rule that can govern the application of the rules." But it disengages the regression in a manner quite different from that suggested by Hobbes: far from anchoring the application of the rules to the exit from the state of nature, Wittgenstein places natural life at the very heart of historically determined institutions.

The *state of nature* merges with the *regularity* of species-specific behaviors. The *civil state* is defined, instead, by the coupling *rule/application*. The "natural" regularity does not cease, not even for a moment, to interfere with both of the terms of the "civil" coupling, equally with the application as with the rule. First of all, as we have seen, because the application is never unequivocally inferable from the corresponding rule, it always, to a certain degree, abides by regularity. Furthermore, because regularity is the anthropological background that allows for the modification of the rules enforced up to this point, or allows us to introduce the rules again. In order to synthesize into a single phrase these two concomitant aspects, one could say: deciding how to realize the norm in a contingent occasion requires the same wisdom, that is to say, the same familiarity with "the common behavior of mankind," as is necessary to establish a norm *ex novo*. Even if the double identification of natural state = regularity, civil state = rule/application, is only partly correct, it is believable that every application of a rule inside the civil state implies a return to the natural state. Better yet: it is believable that the caesura between the two environments lacks any foundation.

Theories of sovereignty completely separate regularity, which is the prejuristic arrangement of the forms of life, from positively determined rules and, above all, from their application in this or that particular case. The *rules without regularity* of the civil state stand in opposition to the *regularity without rules* of the natural state. If it is cut off from true and real rules, regularity is certainly risky and unstable: the ambivalence of the neotenic animal is thus reduced to its aggressive side alone. If they are cut off from regularity, positive rules turn out to be unquestionable and they demand, in order to be observed, a preliminary pact of obedience whose power is indifferent to the normative content in question from time to time. The concrete application of civil rules, unable to make reference to "the common behavior of mankind" (that is, to the environment that precedes the norms and makes possible their definition), resembles, perforce, a compulsion to repeat. Here we recall Freud: "[institutional] order is a kind of compulsion to repeat which, when a regulation has been laid down once and for all, decides when, where, and how a thing shall be done, so that in every similar circumstance one is spared hesitation and indecision" (Freud, *Civilization*: 46). This compulsion to repeat must not be criticized in the name of an imaginary predisposition toward accord and friendship on the part of *Homo sapiens*. On the contrary, one of the grave defects of the compulsion to repeat (not its only defect, let it be understood) is its inability to contain the dangerous (self)destruction of our species. To say nothing of those cases in which it is exactly the compulsion to repeat that stirs up (self)destruction or brings it to its diapason. A theory of institutions that seeks to abandon the paradigm of sovereignty, without eluding the question of intraspecies aggression, must place at center stage that inviolable weaving together of the three levels on which human praxis is articulated: a) regularity, or "the common behavior of mankind"; b) defined rule; c) application contingent upon the defined rule. None of these levels (and even less so, the application) constitutes a free zone, immune from so called "evil": all these levels are a theatre for the oscillation between the good life and the Superdome of New Orleans.

3. The Impossibility of Leaving the Natural State

The crisis of the central modern State, for which Carl Schmitt already expressed regret, as far back as the 1960s, depends to a large extent upon the intervening impossibility of carving out *pseudoenvironments* more or less circumscribed, within the center of which the praxis of the linguistic animal would be exempt from that undifferentiated potentiality that the "opening to the world" always brings with it. This is a *technical* impossibility, above all. The "opening to the world," and, consequently, a certain grade of undifferentiated potentiality, really constitutes the outstanding requisite of today's productive activity. The working process based on knowledge and linguistic communication, just like the forms of life subjected to perpetual innovation, presupposes the capacity of moving from well defined *rules* to a bioanthropological *regularity*, and then from regularity back to the rules, in a ceaseless wavering. In the absence of an explicit reference to the "common behavior of mankind," the application of a rule in a particular circumstance could not even begin to take place. This is even more the case if the contingent application coincides frequently, as happens today, with a partial modification of the specific norm from which it arises. The crisis of the central modern State derives, therefore, from the impossibility of separating political rules from species-specific regularity. But since the regularity has historically taken on the name of "natural state," one could also say: this crisis derives from the *impossibility of leaving the natural state.*

The prominence attained by regularity, that is by the "opening to the world" (neoteny, excessive drive, condition of the possible, etc.), at the center of the contemporary public sphere is such that the functioning of the institutions can be characterized, here and now, as a *permanent state of exception.* Here is the function and content of the state of exception as proclaimed by the sovereign: allowing the regularity that lies below the rules to emerge for a moment (in the words of Schmitt: "the normal structure of the relationships of life" upon which norms rest), and then allowing the political decision to take root directly in this extrajuristic terrain. Yet, in an era in which regularity remains always in full view as the orienting criterion of praxis, the state of exception becomes routine; moreover, far from still being an exclusive prerogative of the sovereign, its proclamation reenters the quotidian experience of every single linguistic animal. It is quite true that the permanent state of exception manifests itself, today, for the most part, as an exceptional permanence of state sovereignty and as an extension *sine die* of the preliminary pact of obedience. But it is also true that the chronic state of exception shows, when held up to the light, the possibility of objecting to the workings of sovereignty as a whole, by embarking on an exodus whose dignity is entrusted to the capacity for confronting the *murmurings*, the dangerous instability of our species, beyond the "monopoly of political decision-making."

Let us consider those salient aspects of the state of exception from which one can deduce the form and functioning of political institutions that are no longer of the State. The state of exception, it has been said, emphasizes, for a brief lapse of time, the regularity underlying the rules that are positively determined. So then, the political institutions of the exodus find their center of gravity in the constant exhibition of the relationship between regularity and rules. This is a bidirectional relationship: the controversial application of the rules calls regularity into question, and regularity, in turn, allows for the formation of new rules. This coming and going, which in the theory of sovereignty is an eventuality both limited and paroxysmal, constitutes, instead, the osseous structure of a Republic in which the monopoly of decision making might be shattered. Regularity, which the institutions of the exodus metabolize, is ambivalent, even perturbing: the opening to the world, negation, the modality of the possible, present themselves, at one and the same time, both as maximum danger and as an authentic resource for warding off evil. Regularity is the environment in which the act of distinguishing clearly between questions of rights and questions of fact, between *grammatical* propositions (positive norms) and empirical propositions (referring to concrete actions), is not always a given. Wittgenstein writes: "It might be imagined that some propositions, of the form of empirical propositions, were hardened and functioned as channels for such *empirical* propositions as were not hardened but fluid; and that this relation altered with time, in that fluid propositions hardened, and hard ones became fluid" (Wittgenstein, *Certainty*:

§ 15e). So then, regularity is defined precisely by this double conversion on the basis of which "the fluid propositions [the factual ones] solidify [that is, take on normative features], and the rigid propositions [the norms] become fluid [factual]." In the normal structuring of the relations of life, or in the behavior common to mankind, the *semisolid or semifluid propositions* prevail: these propositions demonstrate both the tone contingent upon rules, and the regulative extent of contingent actions.

The political institutions that interject the relationship between regularity and rules, thus recognizing the impossibility of leaving the natural state, find their own fundamental principle, or plausible *Magna Charta*, in another affirmation of Wittgenstein: "the same proposition may be treated at one time as something to test by experience, at another as a rule of testing" (ibid: 98). Many and detailed are the rules one must obey in a disciplined manner during the course of the exodus, but among these rules there is not one that, in the moment in which its application becomes controversial, is able to avoid being "controlled" like any empirical proposition whatsoever. The rule is controlled and, if such be the case, revoked and substituted with a different norm. The fact that every rule, standing out against the background of regularity, can be both instrument *and* object of control, is the political, even *constitutional*, equivalent of the ambivalence that distinguishes the linguistic animal. The risky intraspecies aggression, embedded in this fundamental ambivalence, can be held in check only by a *second degree ambivalence*: precisely the one that allows for perceiving, in the "rule of testing," a proposition that "needs to be tested." The political duplication of ambivalence alone, and certainly not its elimination from the civil state, is able to confront the undoubted dangerousness of "'a being capable of creating distance' who in his essence is undetermined, unfathomable, and remains an 'open question'" (Schmitt, *Concept*: 60).

The *multitude*, defamed by Hobbes, who judged it to be a mere regurgitation of the state of nature within the civil state, this *multitude* constitutes, today, the fundamental form of political existence. It is no longer an incidental parenthesis, but a stable way of being. In an era when the modern State is waning, and the "monopoly of political decision making" is falling to pieces, it happens that in every aspect of social organization a plurality of individuals prone to avoid (and even, at times, to obstruct) the circuits of representative democracy becomes ever more valid. This is a plurality that at times is aggressive, and at times united, but never reducible to the concept of the "populous," a populous that, according to Hobbes, "is somewhat that is *one*, having one will" (Hobbes, *Citizen*: 135). Sometimes aggressive, sometimes united, prone to intelligent cooperation, but also to the war between factions, being both the poison and the antidote: such is the multitude. It adequately embodies the three key-words with which, a little while earlier, we tried to clarify what might be a nondialectic understanding of the negative: ambivalence, oscillation, that which is perturbing.

The contemporary multitude exhibits, in and of itself, within its own concrete behavior, the connection between regularity and rule, not to mention the partial indistinctness between questions of rights and questions of fact, grammatical propositions and empirical propositions. The multitude is a *historiconatural* category. In fact, it suits the *historical* situation in which all the distinctive traits of human *nature*, beginning with the articulation between drives and language, have earned an immediate political relevance. The "many" introduce uncertainty into the public sphere, and also the undifferentiated potential of the animal that, being deprived of an environmental niche, is open to the world. We know that the multitude is opposed to the people, to their "one will." It would be a mistake, however, to believe that the multitude can dispose of the One as such. The exact opposite is true: the political existence of the "many," in as much as the word "many" presupposes something of a community, is rooted in a homogeneous and shared environment, and stands out against an impersonal background. The One, from which the "many" become a community, is certainly not state sovereignty; rather, it is the conglomerate of species-specific faculties (verbal thought, cognitive aptitudes, imagination, the ability to learn, etc.) that the history of big industry has tossed onto center stage, to the point of making of these faculties the genuine mainstay of modern production. We might say: the One which the "many" always carry on their backs coincides in many aspects with that *transindividual* reality that Marx called *general intellect* or "social brain" (Marx, *Grundisse*: 694). The *general intellect* is the name that refers to the ordinary human faculty of thinking with words, and this, in turn, becomes the principal productive force of mature capitalism. The *general intellect* is a peculiar historical concretion of regularity, or the "common behavior of mankind," that, according to Wittgenstein, precedes the determined rules and thus functions as the final criterion for their application. The One of the "many" is not different, then, from the regularity that stimulates the behavior of the disoriented animal; or we can say that it is not something different from the opening to the world itself. We should add, however, that regularity and the opening to the world represent the One of the "many" in the precise and exclusive measure to which they are raised historically to the rank of real and true *technicoproductive resources*.

Let us recall the words with which Hobbes deprecated the "irregular political systems" that reflect the multitude's way of being, referring to them as nothing but "leagues, or sometimes mere concourse of people, without union to any particular design, not by obligation of one to another." (Hobbes, *Leviathan*: 154). These irregular political systems, or better yet, their equivalents in today's world, must be viewed as a decisive *experimentum crucis*. It is worth it here to make an observation about terminology: these political systems seem "irregular" to theoreticians of sovereignty precisely because they provide an institutional expression for the *regularity* lying beneath the rules. For Hobbes, the "leagues" and "concourses" are inconsistent in their application of (or eventually, in their failure to apply) the current laws in force on the strength of that extrajuristic parameter that is the "common behavior of mankind." These organisms, which one could call the institutions of the multitude, tend to confer a *political* statute on the "general intellect," on species-specific regularity, on the opening to the world: that is, on all that which unites a plurality of singles, on the One of the "many" that, until now, however, presented itself only in the form of a *technico-productive* resource. Moreover, we have reason to believe that the "leagues, or sometimes mere concourse of people, without union to any particular design, not by obligation of one to another" are the only guarantee for the *ambivalence of the second degree* of which we spoke earlier; the same holds for the politicoinstitutional system truly capable of smoothing out and containing the congenital dangerousness of the linguistic animal. It is only within these concourses, in fact, that "the same proposition may be treated at one time as something to test by experience, at another as a rule of testing" (Wittgenstein, *Certainty*, 98). This politico-institutional ambivalence, according to which every norm appears as both an instrument *and* as an object of control, this is what truly counts in the course of an exodus that is never exempt from murmurings.

3

Historiconatural Institutions

Since the human animal presents a high rate of instability and of intraspecies aggression, it is useful to develop, all the way to its extreme consequences, a critique of the modern State (and of the capitalist mode of production). In the preceding pages I attempted to render this unusual inference plausible. Not only does "hostile radicalism towards the State" not hesitate to recognize the (self)destructive drives of living animals endowed with language; it takes those drives so seriously as to judge their antidote, proposed by the theories of sovereignty, as being unrealistic, and even extremely harmful. Every other polemical issue aside, it seems evident that the preliminary agreement to obedience and the connected compulsion to repeat, in the application of civic rules, do not assure any effective protection from the risks inherent in the opening to the world and in the process of neoteny. Not withstanding a certain assertive, if peremptory, tone, the discussion, as it has been developed to this point, maintains the character of conjecture. If the hypothesis is wise, it leads us to discussion, and nothing more than this. Sometimes the facts just don't add up. The philosophical analysis of danger that distinguishes the linguistic animal is too fragile; the study of certain delicate problems of political theory has been simplified to the point of something of a caricature. Nonetheless, when we are not able to respect the numerous debts accrued in the process of our analysis, there is only one thing we can do: count up these debts again, willingly accepting that the very nature of our analysis is insoluble.

Rather than closing ranks, I prefer to open up a bit more the field of investigation. In this final section of my essay, I would like to lay bare some further conjectures on the form and function of political organisms that end up being incompatible with the "monopoly of the political decision," even when they are confronted up close with the fearful aspects of human nature. Let us establish the questions that will serve as the thread of our analysis. Which institutions faithfully reflect the impossibility of escaping the state of nature and, precisely for this reason, give evidence of the comings and goings between species-specific regularity and definitive rules? Which institutions exhibit, through their normal mode of functioning, the reciprocal commutability between grammatical propositions and empirical propositions—that commutability which, according to the theories of sovereignty, affirms itself only within the state of exception? Which institutions metabolize ambivalence and oscillation, rather than postulating their unilateral resolution? And which institutions, finally, avoid the delineation of a pseudoenvironment for human praxis, thus meriting the designation of being truly *worldly* institutions?

I will attempt now to respond to these questions without making further reference to that which *could be*; rather, I will focus my attention on that which *has always been*. In other words, I will ignore for a moment the necessity of inventing political categories that can be considered social transformations in progress, so as to concentrate on two macroscopic anthropological—actually, *anthropogenetic*—realities that are, for all practical purposes, institutions: language and ritual. These are precisely the institutions that exhibit most clearly the requirements for answering the questions I have listed above: the assertion of the reciprocal commutability between issues concerning rights and issues concerning fact, the intimacy of ambivalence and oscillation. These two historiconatural institutions, which I will analyze only in minimal and indispensable detail, are *not*, however, political institutions. Nonetheless, we must not exclude the possibility of tracing within our tradition one or more conceptual signs that can represent the actual political equivalent of language and of ritual. Within our tradition: even here, as we see, I am not invoking what is yet to come; I am speaking of what has already been. As far as ritual is concerned, I propose the following hypothesis: the manner in which ritual continuously confronts and mitigates the dangerous instability of the human animal has its equivalent in the theologicopolitical category of *katechon*. This Greek word, used by the apostle Paul in his Second Epistle to the Thessalonians and then constantly referred to in conservative doctrine, means "that which restrains"—a force that defers, over and over again, total destruction. It seems to me that the concept of *katechon*, with the political implication of ritual practices, contributes significantly in defining the structure and the duties of institutions that no longer pertain to the state. The idea of a force that restrains so-called "evil," without the possibility of expelling this evil (since that would correspond to the end of the world, or to the atrophy of the "opening to the world"), falls within the framework of the antimonopolistic politics of the exodus. This idea is far from being an intrinsic element of the theory of sovereignty, as Schmitt and company would have it.

Language, ritual, *katechon*: these are nothing more than notes written in the margins of an essay whose plausible conclusion lies within the sphere of reflections on the ambivalence of the second degree, which pertains principally to the institutions of the multitude (See above: § 2.3). The final pages of my essay, where we open up once again the discussion of what has already been discussed, certainly give the impression of being extemporaneous. This is fine: the centrifugal and dispersive nature of these pages will enable us to show, without further feigning, the conjectural and halting nature of my entire analysis.

1. Language

Language has a preindividual and superindividual life. It concerns the single human animal only in as much as this animal is part of a "mass of speakers." Just like freedom or power, it exists only in the relation *between* the members of a community. Bifocal vision, the autonomous heritage of every isolated human being, can rightly be considered to be a shared prerogative of the species. Not so for language. In the case of language, it is the sharing that creates the prerogative; and it is the *between* of the interpsychic relationship that determines, by means of mirroring, an intrapsychic heritage. Historiconatural language attests to the priority of the "we" over the "I," of the collective mind over the individual mind. For this reason, we can never repeat Saussure enough in saying that language is an institution. It is for this reason precisely that language is the "pure institution," the matrix and touchstone of all the other institutions.

Such a judgment would not be justified, however, if language, in addition to being superpersonal, did not also have an integrative and protective function. But what is the gap that this historiconatural language must fill? And from what risk must it protect us? Both gap and risk have an exact name: the faculty of language. This faculty, or biological disposition, in the case of a single individual, is simply a potentiality that is still lacking an effective reality, far too similar to a state of aphasia. Saussure writes: "Nature gives us man *ready made for articulated language,* but *not actually in possession of it.* The *language system* is a social fact. The individual, organized with a view to speaking, may only use the vocal apparatus in the context of his community—moreover, the individual only feels the need to use it when interacting with that community. [...] In this respect, then, the human being is whole only through what he borrows from society" (Saussure: 120). Language, as social fact or pure institution, provides the remedy to individual *infancy,* to that condition in which one does not speak even when one is in possession of the capacity for language. Language protects the neotenic animal from the greatest of dangers to which it can be exposed: an ability that remains simply an ability, lacking in corresponding actions. The difference between the faculty of language and historically determined languages confers an institutional tonality upon the natural life of our species; this difference, far from healing itself, persists even into adulthood, making itself evident every time someone produces an utterance. It is exactly this difference that implies an extremely strong connection between biology and politics, between *zoon logon ekon* and *zoon politikon.*

Language is the institution that renders all other institutions possible: fashion, marriage, law, the State, and so on. But the matrix is radically distinguished from its by-products. According to Saussure, the functioning of language can not be compared to that of law or to that of the State. The unquestionable analogies reveal themselves to be deceptive. The transformation in time of the civil code has nothing in common with the consonant change or alteration of certain lexical values. The gap that separates the "pure institution" from the sociopolitical apparatus with which we are familiar is, perhaps, quite instructive for our investigation. By continuing to employ the terminology that we have established to this point, one can only say that language is effectively a *worldly* institution; *worldly* in such a way as to reflect, in its very mode of being, the overabundance of stimuli not yet finalized biologically, not to mention the chronic "detachment" of the human animal with regard to its own living context. Let us read two crucial passages from Saussure:

> *Langue* as a social phenomenon can be compared with *customs* (constitution, law, habits, etc.). Art and religion are further afield, being manifestations of mind in which personal initiative plays a large part, and which do not presuppose an exchange between two individuals. But the analogy with 'customs' is itself highly relative. [...] Language, belonging to the community, like 'tradition', corresponds in the individual to a special organ primed by nature. This fact, in itself, bears no analogy (ibid: 120).
>
> [Language] is a human institution, but, by its very nature, any unfortunate analogy with any other human institution, *except writing*, can only misrepresent its real essence. This is because the other institutions are to various degrees all based on NATURAL relationships [...]. For instance, a nation's *laws*, or political system, or even fashion, even its whimsical sartorial fashions, which can never ignore the given [proportions] of the human body. It follows that all changes,

all innovations [...] are always dependent on the basic principle in force in this very area, which is to be found in the very depths of the human soul. But language and writing are NOT BASED on a natural relationship between things. There is never a way to link a certain sibilant sound and the shape of the letter *S*, and similarly it is no harder for the word *vache* than the word *vacca* to refer to a cow. [...]. Language is nothing other than an institution. But it proves much more; it shows that language is an institution which has no COMPARABLE COUNTERPART (ibid: 146–147).

Language is also more natural and more historical than any other institution. *More natural*: unlike the world of fashion or of the State, the foundation of language lies in a "special organ prepared by nature," or in that innate biological disposition that is the faculty of language. *More historical*: while marriage and law fit into the category of certain natural givens (sexual desire and the raising of children, for the former; symmetry of exchanges and proportionality between damage and compensation, for the latter), language is never bound to one or the other objective sphere, but it concerns the entire experience of the animal open to the world—the possible no less than the real—the unknown—as well as the habitual. Fashion can not be located in a cerebral area and yet it must always respect the proportions of the human body. Quite to the contrary, language depends on certain genetic conditions, even though it has an unlimited field of application (since, in and of itself, it can continuously broaden this field). Let us quote Saussure once again: "Whether in clothing or [...], the natural relationship between things is always reasserted after an aberration and remains the driving entity throughout the ages, one which through all the changes remains the rule. The processes of language, however, within language's allotted function among human institutions, are bereft of any limit whatsoever [...]; language may not be accounted for within a human rule, which is continually corrected or directed or is able to be corrected or directed by human reason" (ibid: 149). Language, reflecting the typically human lack of a circumscribed and foreseeable environment, is "deprived of any limit whatsoever" in its processes. But what offers clear protection with regard to the risks connected to the typically human deficit is precisely this unlimited variability of language, or its independence from factual circumstances and natural data.

The pure institution, being both the most natural and the most historical, is also, however, a *nonsubstantial* institution. Saussure's fixed idea on this is well known: there is no positive reality in language, one that is endowed with autonomous consistency. There are only differences and differences between differences. Every term is defined by "the degree to which it does not coincide with the rest" (ibid: 153); in other words, by opposition or heterogeneity with respect to all other terms. The value of a linguistic element that consists in its *not being*: x is something only because it is not y, nor z, nor w, etc. The ability of the speaker to negate one or another state of worldly things (at times deactivating even perceptive evidence) is limited to taking back and exteriorizing the "complex of eternally negative differences" (ibid: 153) that has always characterized the interior life of language. The negation, or something that language *does*, is understood, above all, as something that language *is*. The pure institution does not *represent* any force or reality already given; rather, it can only *signify* this force or reality, thanks to the negative-differential relationship that operates among its components. The pure institution is neither the spokesperson nor the mold of anything; in this manner, language displays its consubstantiality with "a being capable of creating distance."

Can we conceive of an institution that is *political*, in the strictest sense of this adjective, if that institution changes its own form and function by means of language? Is it plausible to have a Republic that protects and stabilizes the human animal in the same way in which language performs its protective and stabilizing role with respect to the faculty of language, to neoteny? A nonrepresentative, insubstantial, Republic based upon differences and differences between differences? I cannot answer this. Just like anyone else, I distrust dazzling allusions and speculative short circuits. Above all, when we need to confront and evaluate ourselves with regard to the event that took place in the Superdome in New Orleans. I maintain, however, that the current crisis of State sovereignty legitimizes such questions, eliminating from them any leisurely or pleasing nuance. Whether the self-government of the multitude can adapt itself directly to the linguistic aspect of the human species, to the disturbing ambivalence that characterizes this linguistic aspect, will have to remain an open problem.

2. Ritual

Ritual records and confronts every sort of crisis: the uncertainty that paralyzes action, the dread of the unknown, the intensification of aggressive drives within a community. In the most significant cases, the crisis with which ritual occupies itself does not refer, however, to this or that determined form of behavior, even though it supplies the same conditions for possibilities of experience: the unity of self-knowledge and the opening to the world. Ernesto de

Martino uses the term "crisis of presence" for those neuralgic occasions on which the Ego disintegrates and the world seems to be on the brink of collapse. What manifests itself clearly, in such predicaments, is the partial reversibility of the anthropogenetic process. That is to say, the possession of those fundamental requirements that make a human animal a human animal becomes uncertain. Ritual fulfills a therapeutic function not because it erects a barrier against the "crisis of presence," but because, on the contrary, it goes back over each stage of the crisis and tries to overturn the traces of each of those stages. Ritual praxis upholds extreme danger, widens uncertainty and chaos, and returns to the primal setting of the original hominid. In this way alone, moreover, can ritual action perform a symbolic repetition of anthropogensesis, reaffirming, in the end, the unity of the Ego and the opening to the world. According to de Martino, the psychopathological collapse and the catastrophe of the associated life are held in check by "cultural apocalypses," or by the collective rituals that imitate destruction in order to repel it. Cultural apocalypses are institutions based upon *ambivalence* and *oscillation*. This is an ambivalence of the critical situations in which only loss can offer the possibility of redemption, and there is no other remedy except for that which danger itself delineates. The oscillation is a movement between something familiar that becomes agitated and something agitated that ends up emitting familiarity.

The crisis of presence has two opposing and symmetrical courses. It can consist of a painful "defect of semanticity"—but also, inversely, of an uncontrollable, ever-expanding whirlwind caused by an "excess of semanticity that can not be resolved with absolute meanings" (Martino: 89). The *defect of semanticity* is ultimately the reduction of human discourse to a defined series of monotonous signals. The Ego contracts into a mass of stereotyped behaviors: the compulsory repetition of the same formulas and gestures prevails; the world dries up and is simplified to the point of resembling a papier-mâché backdrop. The *excess of semanticity*, on the other hand, is equivalent to a state of shapeless potentiality. We witness a progressive loss of definition of the word; discourse, having been released from unambiguous references, takes on the responsibility of an "obscure allusiveness." The Ego is reabsorbed in a chaotic world whose fundamental elements, still far from constituting discrete unities, are, rather, based upon an unstable and contained continuum. This world is characterized by acts without power, in the case of the "defect of semanticity," and by power without acts, in the case of the "excess of semanticity." These are the symmetrical ways in which one is made to see the regression of the anthropogenetic process, or, in the words of de Martino, the risk of "the end of the world." Nonetheless, in reference to considerations that have already been discussed (see above: § 2.2), one might also say: the defect of semanticity corresponds to a unity of *rules detached from species-specific regularities*, the application of which takes on the appearance of an instinctive reflex, or, better yet, of coercion towards repetition. The excess of semanticity, for its part, coincides with a *regularity free of rules*, dominated by an unhampered polysemy and by undifferentiated drives. The rules are never really the way they seem to be if they are separated from a preliminary regularity (or "from the normal structuring of vital relationships"). The situation is such that one cannot speak about an authentic regularity where there is no trace of defined rules. The crisis of presence, or the atrophy of the opening to the world, exasperates the risks implied in the polarity of natural state / civil state that constitutes the hinge of state sovereignty. The civil state, by guaranteeing the automatic application of the norms in force, is distinguished by a defect of semanticity; the natural state, with its frightful regularity without rules, is affected, instead, by a constant excess of semanticity.

We know that cultural apocalypses, for de Martino, are the rituals in which we experience, in the most acute manner, the collapse of the opening to the world and, *at the same time*, the restoration of the norm. We also know that these institutions are marked by ambivalence: they provide protection by making use of the same conditions that give birth to danger. "It is necessary to understand that, with respect to 'meaning,' the same behavior can occur twice in the same individual person: as a symptom of crisis and as a symbol of reintegration" (ibid: 174). The cultural apocalypses illustrate the anthropogenetic threshold in which it is difficult to trace a clear distinction between "never again" and "not yet," between continued loss and the beginning of redemption. In these apocalypses, the separation between potential and act is confirmed—in fact, this leads to the diapason: for the sake of reaffirming, however, their customary intertwining. Those who find themselves living a cultural apocalypse are made to experience the "defect of semanticity," together with the stereotyped actions and signal-phrases that accompany this defect; they are made to experience, equally, the mirror "excess of semanticity that can not be resolved in precise terms," together with the consequent predominance of a shapeless potentiality. But they experience that defect (regulations without regularity) and excess (regularity without regulations) as an act of restabilizing, from scratch, the peculiar conditions of possibility that discourse and praxis entail.

The cultural apocalypse is the ritualistic counterpart of the state of exception. This even implies the suspension of ordinary laws, thus allowing certain salient characteristics of human nature to emerge (crisis and the repetition of the same anthropogenetic process) within a particular historical junction. Just like the state of exception, the cultural apocalypse also delineates an environment in which it is possible to discern, without any hesitation, the grammatical plane from the empirical, the general rule from the singular application, issues of law from issues of fact. The cultural apocalypse, just like the sate of exception, is such that every normative proposition shows itself to be, also, an instrument of control and a reality to be controlled, a unit of measure and a measurable phenomenon. We have seen, however, that the state of exception has become, in our era, the stable condition of common life (see above: § 2.3). It is no longer a circumscribed interval, instituted and formalized by the sovereign; it is instead a permanent tonality of action and discourse. This conflict is valid also for ritual. The cultural apocalypse does not remain confined within a special time or space; it concerns all aspects of contemporary experience. The motive is simple. The institutional task of ritual consists of containing the risks to which the *opening to the world* of the linguistic animal is subjected. Thus, during the period when the opening to the world is no longer veiled or blunted by social pseudoenvironments (when it truly represents a fundamental technical resource), this task must be performed without any interruption. The oscillation between the loss of presence and its act of reestablishing itself characterizes every aspect of social praxis. The ambivalence between symptoms of crisis and symbols of redemption pervade the average everyday life.

We are left, then, to ask ourselves if the cultural apocalypse, the historiconatural institution that serves as a leash for controlling oscillation and ambivalence, has a strictly political equivalent—if ritual, in addition to widening itself within all the interstices of profane time, provides also some information on the possible functioning of a Republic that is no longer politicojuristic. My answer to these questions is affirmative. As I have already explained, I maintain that the ancient concept of *katechon*, the "force that restrains," constitutes the plausible political equivalent of cultural apocalypses; and that this concept, just as is the case for a cultural apocalypse, is in no way absolutely tied to the vicissitudes of State sovereignty.

3. Katechon

In his Second Epistle to the Thessalonians, the apostle Paul speaks of a force that restrains the prevalence of evil in the world, continually keeping at bay the triumph of the Antichrist. Holding back, restraining: these are terms that have nothing in common with "expunging" or "defeating" or even "circumscribing." That which restrains does not distance itself from what needs to be restrained; rather, it remains close to it and does not even avoid mingling with what must be restrained. *Katechon* does not eradicate evil, but it does limit it, and it wards off repeatedly every blow that evil presents. It does not save us from destruction, but it restrains destruction and, in order to restrain it, it conforms to the innumerable occasions when destruction can manifest itself. It resists the pressure of chaos by adhering to chaos, just as the concave adheres to the convex. The boundary between *katechon* does not pertain exclusively to either of the two adversaries. Just as we saw in the ritualistic device described by Ernesto de Martino, this line of demarcation is, also, a symptom of the crisis and of its redemption, an expression of the iniquity and the physiological aspect of virtue. Or perhaps it is better to say that it is something only because it is something else.

In medieval and modern political thought, *katechon* has been identified, first of all, with the secular power of the Church, and then with the centripetal institutions of the sovereign State, that, by imposing a preliminary pact of obedience, sought to oppose the breakup of the social body. Here is what Carl Schmitt writes in *The Nomos of the Earth*: "The Christian Empire was not eternal. It always had its own end and that of the present eon in view. Nevertheless, it was capable of being a historical power. The decisive historical concept of this continuity was that of the restrainer: *katechon*. 'Empire,' in this sense meant the historical power to *restrain* the appearance of the Antichrist and the end of the present eon" (Schmitt, *Nomos*: 59–60). Certainly this is not the time to discuss in detail the conservative and state-worshiping use of the notion of *katechon*. For the moment, a singular observation will suffice: Schmitt and his family photo album (Hobbes, de Maistre, Donoso Cortés) call forth a "force that restrains" in order to indicate *generically* the stabilizing and protective role that competes with political institutions in the face of the danger confronted by the disoriented and neotenic animal. Such a role is fundamental, but not extenuating. It can claim responsibility, in principle, for the most diverse variations of the political institution (let us clarify here that this can occur by means of communal anarchy and also by means of a military dictatorship), or even for innumerable non-political institutions (beginning with language and ritual). As it is understood in its most common meaning, *katechon* is a ubiquitous and pervasive property, perhaps a bioanthropological constant. The salient point, for Schmitt and for writers of his ilk, is not at all the call to a "force that restrains." Rather, it is an unambiguous attribution to sovereignty. The question of *katechon* is once again compromised when one postulates an institutional protection for it, thus denying that the State and the connected "monopoly of political decision-making" can guarantee this protection (given that these forces can constitute the highest level of danger). Since dissimilar modes are in a state of competition here, or even poles apart from each other (in terms of containing the risky instability of the linguistic animal), it seems appropriate not only to detach the idea of *katechon* from the "supreme empire" of the state, but also to place one notion in opposition to the other. It is obvious that all of this does not hold true for those who criticize the State while maintaining confidence in the innate gentility of our species. For such persons, a "force that restrains" is always something worthy of blame; for these people, then, the appropriation of *katechon* on behalf of authoritarian political thought is absolutely legitimate, and even irrefutable. But I would like to forget about such people.

If we equate the concept of *katechon* with the apotropaic function innate in any political (and nonpolitical) institution, we will have to conclude that the concept of *katechon* surpasses and exceeds the concept of state sovereignty: between the two concepts there exists an unfillable gap, the same gap that separates the genus from the species, the syntagm "linguistic animal" from the syntagm "university professor." If, instead, we turn our attention to the truly peculiar characteristics of *katechon*, to that which makes up this very word, it will not be difficult to ascertain its radical heterogeneity in the form of protection presented by state sovereignty (that hinges, as we know, upon the exit from the state of nature and the preliminary pact of obedience). Let us now choose this second path. In order to grasp the characteristic aspects of *katechon* as a political institution, those aspects that link it to cultural apocalypses and place it in opposition to the modern central State, it is necessary to give our attention for a moment to the theological warp of *katechon*.

Katechon is characterized by internal antynomy. This force keeps in check both radical evil and protean aggression. But, according to the book of the *Apocalypse*, the triumph of the Antichrist constitutes the necessary premise for the coming of the Messiah, for the *parousia* who will save everyone forever and put an end to the world. Here is the double bond to which *katechon* is subjected: if it restrains evil, it blocks the final defeat of evil; if it limits aggression, it gets in the way of having this aggression annihilated once and for all. Thwarting continuously the dangerous state of the species *Homo sapiens* means, of course, avoiding its lethal unleashing; but it also means, and perhaps more importantly, prohibiting the definitive elimination of that dangerous state: that elimination, let us understand, which the theories of sovereignty pursue by means of a sharp division between the state of nature and the civil state. From a logical perspective, the antynomy that takes root in the *katechon*-institution is comparable, perhaps, to the paradoxical command: "I command you to be spontaneous!": if I am spontaneous, then I am not spontaneous, since I am following the command to be so; if I follow the command, I am not really following it, while being spontaneous. From a logical perspective, this same antynomy becomes as productive as ever, delineating a model of institutional protection according to which the (auto)destructive drives connected to the opening to the world can be confronted, thanks only to the same bio-linguistic conditions (neoteny, negation, modalities of the possible, etc.) that are the foundation and guarantee of this opening. In brief, it protects from risk only that state whose existence it preserves. This notion is completely in agreement with what Roberto Esposito writes in the pages of his *Immunitas* that are dedicated to the figure of the *katechon*: it "restrains evil by containing it, maintaining it, detaining it within itself [...], hosting it and welcoming it to the point of binding to its very presence its very necessity" (Esposito: 116).

Let us repeat the focal point of our argument. By impeding the triumph of the Antichrist, *katechon* impedes, at the same time, the redemption to be accomplished by the Messiah. Restraining iniquity involves the renunciation of the pristine state of innocence. *Katechon*, a radically antieschatological and theologicopolitical concept, is opposed to the "end of the world," or, better yet, to the atrophy of the opening to the world, to the various ways in which the crisis of presence can be made manifest. Both victorious evil and complete victory over evil lead to the same end, that is to say, to the state of atrophy. *Katechon* protects us from the deadly instability that emanates from the Antichrist , but that emanates equally from the messianic state of equilibrium; from terrifying instability, and equally from the redeeming entropy. In strict analogy with cultural apocalypses, *katechon* brings into check two fundamental forms of the crisis of presence: the *excess of semanticity* (that state of undifferentiated potential in which omnilateral violence takes its form) and the *defect of semanticity* (the compulsion to repeat, which is the stereotype of behaviors and of discourse). By placing itself in opposition to danger and also to the elimination of that danger, to the Antichrist and also to the Messiah, the *katechon* delays the end of the world. But the opening to the world, the stigma of the linguistic animal, consists precisely in this constantly renewed deferral. Just as presence itself is nothing more than a constant redemption from the crisis of presence, so too, the nature of *anthropos* is equal to the regression and repetition of anthropogenesis. *Katechon* not only oscillates between the negative and the positive, without ever expunging the negative; it also safeguards the state of oscillation and its persistence as such.

In strictly political terms, *katechon* is the republican institution in charge of foiling the two catastrophic eventualities that can radically undermine social interaction: the case in which the regularity of species-specific behaviors becomes prominent, though deprived of any determined rule (excess of semanticity); and also the case, opposite and yet symmetrical, in which a system of rules is in force, rules that deviate from regularity, demanding an automatic and uniform application (defect of semanticity). These catastrophic eventualities correspond, as we know, to the separation between the state of nature (regularity without rules) and the civil state (rules without regularity), from which the theory of sovereignty derives its prestigious title. *Katechon*, therefore, is the republican institution that restrains the risks innate in the instability of a "state of being founded primarily on detachment," which places it in complete contrast to the theory of sovereignty. *Katechon* is the republican institution that holds at bay the risks inherent in the instability of a "being established primarily on the notion of detachment"—in conflict, however, in the same moment, with the quite fearful ways in which the modern State has seen fit to obtain protections from those risks. Just like the normal institutions (Leagues, Councils of State, Assemblies) that characterize the political existence of the multitude, according to Hobbes, *katechon* is tightly bound to circumstances and occasions. There is no signified operative synthesis in place here, with respect to the concrete forms of life, to the powers that be, and to regional conflicts. Rather, *katechon* performs a contingent and punctual task: that of resolving once again the connection between regularity and rules, between "a mode of behavior common to all human beings" and positive norms. This kind of connection, upon which the effective application of rules depends (not to mention the possibility of changing these rules) must be validated over and over again. Since it gives evidence to the relation between regularity and rules, or to the intertwining of natural life and politic praxis, *katechon* is the institution that best adapts itself to the permanent state of exception, to the partial indistinction (or reciprocal commutablility) between the questions of law and the questions of fact, all of which characterize it. It is, then, the institution that best adapts itself to the state of exception, when this state, far from being yet a prerogative of the soverign, indicates rather the action and discourse of the multitude.

In order to understand, in broad terms, the function of *katechon* as a political institution of the multitude, we will need to return once again to verbal language. It is precisely this verbal language that, in fact, represents the maximum source of danger and, also, the authentic restraining force. Let us remind ourselves of the three linguistic structures that reflect the disoriented and neotenic condition of *Homo sapiens*: negation, modality of the possible, and regression to the infinite. All three of these structures, as we have observed (See above: § 1.1) give access to so-called "evil." Negation allows for the overthrowing of reciprocal recognition between members of the same species ("this is *not* a man"). The modality of the possible expresses the scarcity of congenital inhibitions. The regression to the infinite emphasizes the incurable gaps that characterize living beings who lack their own ecological niche. These three structures, in addition to being the root of risk, are also *katechon*, a system of checks, protection.

As far as *negation* is concerned, we have already seen that it can apply itself repeatedly to itself, such that it restores that which it has repealed. The negation of negation ("not not a man") keeps in check the possibility of a reciprocal *non*recognition, thus constituting the implicit presupposition of rhetorical persuasion and, in general, of the permanence of a public sphere. The *modality of the possible* ratifies and foments the formidable lack of inhibition of the human animal; but it also puts protection in place. In the *Prior Analytics*, Aristotle illustrated how the definition of the "possible" is always bidirectional, given that it contains within itself as much the affirmative case as it does the negative: occlusion, no less than opening: something is possible if its inexistence, or even its existence, is not necessary. To assert that "it is possible that X might be" means asserting also that "it is possible that it might not be." The restraint placed upon intraspecies aggression ("it is possible that it might not be") is uniquely based upon that which actually allows it to be. Inhibition, or republican *katechon*, is nourished by the same biolinguistic devices that render the human animal dangerously uninhibited. The *regression to the infinite*, finally, finds its own antidote in the diverse ways in which this regression can be interrupted. We must add, however, that this interruption is efficacious, truly protective, only if it does not limit itself to removing the regression (the true logical counterpart of the lack of an environmental niche). The interruption transforms the regression into a virtuous circle, into a device based upon ambivalence and oscillation. Let us consider once again the unending backward movement that occurs when we are uncertain about the manner in which to apply a rule in a particular situation. Were we to look for another rule, a rule capable of allowing us to understand the previous one, we would need to have recourse to a third rule in order to understand how to apply the second one: and on and on it goes without resolution. This regression can be interrupted by introducing a preliminary pact of obedience to the sovereign. But by doing so, two things occur: the human animal's opening to the world (validated by the never ending "and on and on it goes") is concealed; and a pseudoenvironmental, quite fearful, niche is created. But this same regression can also be interrupted in another way: to be accurate, it translates this "and on and on it goes" within the perpetual *oscillation* between species-specific regularity and established rules. The *ambivalence*, by virtue of which it is appropriate to see a question of fact in every question of law, and in every question of law a question of fact, defines *katechon* as something that restrains (but does not remove) the regression to the infinite.

Earlier in this essay (See above: § 2.3) I maintained that the contemporary multitude is a *historico natural* reality, since it exhibits, in its very mode of being, the peculiar *historical* situation in which all the distinctive traits of human *nature* have earned an immediate political relevance. If this is true, it is necessary to claim also that the contemporary multitude has the greatest level of familiarity with the loss and redemption of presence. Or, we can say that the social existence of the multitude is disseminated by way of those cultural apocalypses in which one experiences both the crisis and the repetition of anthropogenesis. The contemporary multitude reflects within itself, quite apparently, the double ethical value of verbal language: the springing forth of danger and the force that restrains it, radical evil and apotropaic resource. The multitude, just like verbal language, is also a risky state of loss of equilibrium and a favorable restraint: murmurs in the desert and joint self-government, (self)destruction and *katechon*. We might also say: the multitude is negation, and the negation of negation, the uninhibited "it is possible that it might be" and the limiting "it is possible that it might not be": a paralyzing regression to the infinite and its fortunate metamorphosis in political institutions based upon oscillation and ambivalence. The contemporary multitude, in the process of its exodus from state sovereignty, presents to the naked eye the connection between the two renowned Aristotelian definitions of *Homo sapiens*: linguistic animal and political animal.

PART 2

JOKES AND INNOVATIVE ACTION:

FOR A LOGIC OF CHANGE

Prologue

The human animal is capable of modifying its forms of life, of diverging from established rules and customs. If the word "creative" were not undermined by excessive ambiguous misunderstandings, one could also say that the human animal is "creative." This observation, undeniable in and of itself, has nothing to do with the so-called "happy ending": the observation itself, instead, calls forth all sorts of questions and doubts. Of what use are the requirements of praxis and discourse, when we are entering on an unpredictable path? How does the rupture of the state of equilibrium that prevailed until that particular moment occur? When all is said and done, what makes up an innovative action?

There is a tested method for solving the problem, even if such method possesses the air of being involved in the test with nothing to gain. We will have to accept the term "creativity" in its broadest sense, in order for it to be coexistent with the term "human nature." Thus, we arrive, in haste, at some sort of reassuring tautology. The human animal must be capable of innovation because it is gifted with verbal language, or because it lacks a defined and unchanging environment, or because it is a historical phenomenon: in brief, because it is ... a human animal. Applause! Curtain! The tautology avoids the most thorny and interesting point: transformative action is *intermittent*, or even rare. The attempt to explain the statute of tautology, calling into question the distinct characteristics of our species, misses the target, since these characteristics are valid, as is obvious, even when experience is uniform and repetitive.

Chomsky maintains that our language is "constantly innovative," thanks to its independence from "external stimuli or internal states" (Chomsky: 5) and for other reasons that one need not recall here (ibid: 133–170). Fine, but what need is there for this kind of independence, one that encounters no eclipses, and only in certain cases gives way to unusual and surprising verbal performances? It is no surprise that Chomsky, having attributed creativity to language in general (or rather, to "human nature"), concludes that this creativity constitutes a mystery that can not be investigated. Let us consider another example. According to the anthropological philosophy of Arnold Gehlen, *Homo sapiens*, due to its instinctive inexpertise, is always grappling with an overabundance of stimuli that are not biologically finalized, from which unambiguous behaviors cannot descend: this is why the action of Homo sapiens, "unfounded" as it is, can never be not creative (See Gehlen, *Man*: 24–53). Even here the question remains unanswered: how is it that the overabundance of stimuli that are not biologically finalized can give way, for the most part, to stereoptyped operations, and, only rarely, to an unexpected innovation?

It is completely legitimate to deduce from certain defining features of our species the conditions that make possible the variation of behaviors. But it is a blatant error to identify these *conditions of possibility* with the particular *logicolinguistic resources* to which we have recourse when one single behavior undergoes change. There is a gap between the conditions and the resources: the same gap, let it be understood, that separates the *a priori* intuition of space from the inferences by means of which one formulates, or understands, a geometric theorem. The independence of utterances from any "external stimuli or internal states" (Chomsky) and instinctive gullibility (Gehlen) do not explain why the crippled man, when questioned by a blind man who carelessly asks him "How's it going?" responds by lashing out at him, with no small measure of creativity: "Just as you see." Chomsky and Gehlen provide for us only the reasons for which the crippled man *can* react as he does to the involuntary provocation of fate (rather than in many other less surprising ways, such as: "Well, and you?"; "Wonderful"; "Things could be worse"). But Chomsky and Gehlen tell us nothing about the effective procedures that give way to the unexpected swerve in the dialogue. The logicolinguistic resources on which the innovative action relies are more circumscribed, or less generic, than its conditions of possibility. Such resources, even though they are the prerogative of every human animal, are utilized, and achieve their greatest prominence, only on a few critical occasions. Some examples: when a form of life, one that previously seemed incontrovertible, assumes the appearance of an article of clothing too wide or too tight; when the distinction between the "grammatical plane" (the rules of the game) and the "empirical plane" (the facts to which those rules ought to be applied) becomes uncertain; when human praxis, even fleetingly, runs into that difficult logical situation which those versed in law call the *state of exception*.

In order to avoid the risk of the tautology, I propose, then, an acceptance of a very restricted, actually extremely narrow, version of "creativity": the forms of verbal thought that consent to varying their own behavior in an emergency situation. The tautological call to "human nature" does not explain anything: neither the state of equilibrium, nor the act of escaping from this state. Vice versa, an inquiry into the logicolinguistic resources that become preeminent only in the case of crisis, in addition to highlighting the *techniques* of innovation, also casts a different light on repetitive behaviors. It is the unexpected quip of the crippled man that clarifies some salient aspects of the stereotypical responses whose occurrence was much more probable—certainly not the constituent independence of verbal language from environmental and psychological conditioning. The suspension, or modification, of a rule unveils the paradoxes, and its insoluble problems, normally unnoticed, that take root in the most blind and automatic application of the rule.

The following pages concern the concept of jokes. They are guided by the conviction that jokes can offer us an adequate *empirical basis* for understanding the way in which linguistic animals give evidence of an unexpected deviation from their normal praxis. Furthermore, jokes seem to exemplify, quite effectively, the restricted acceptance of "creativity": that is to say, that which does not coincide tautologically with human nature in its complex totality, but uses, instead, a critical situation as its own exclusive testing ground. The principal textual point of reference here is Freud's essay on *Witz*. To my knowledge, there exists no attempt as significant as Freud's to distill a detailed taxonomy, *botanical*, so to speak, of the various kinds of jokes. Freud's deep commitment to identifying those rhetorical figures and patterns of thought that give rise to quick retort is well known. I must inform my reader, however, that my interpretation of the concepts gathered and organized from the work of Freud is rigorously non-Freudian. Rather than dwell upon Freud's eventual affinity for the dream process and the functioning of the unconscious, I wish to emphasize the stringent nexus binding jokes to praxis in the public sphere. It should not be surprising, then, with regard to a successful joke, if I say nothing about dreams and much about *phrónesis*—that is to say, about the practical know-how and the sense of proportion that guide those who act without a safety net in the presence of their equals.

Jokes are the *diagram* of innovative action. By "diagram" I mean, together with Pierce and with the mathematicians, the sign that reproduces in miniature the structure and internal proportions of a certain phenomenon (let us think in terms of an equation or of a map). Jokes are the logicolinguistic diagram of the undertakings that, on the occasion of a historical or biographical crisis, interrupt the circular flux of experience. They are the microcosm in which we witness clearly those mutations of deductive direction and those displacements of meaning that, within the macrocosm of human praxis, provoke the variation of a form of life. Briefly put: jokes are well defined linguistic games, equipped with unique techniques, whose remarkable function consists, however, in *exhibiting the transformability of all linguistic games.*

This general layout of my argument can be articulated in two subordinate hypotheses that need to be enunciated immediately. Let us look at the first of these hypotheses. Jokes have a lot to do with one of the most insidious problems of linguistic praxis: *how to apply a rule to a particular case.* They have a lot to do, on the other hand, precisely with the dangers or the difficulties and uncertainties that sometimes come up in the moment of application. Jokes do not cease to illustrate in how many different, and even contrasting, ways one can comply with the same norm. But it is precisely those divergences emerging through the application of the rule that often bring about the drastic change of the rule itself. Far from positioning itself above or outside the norm, human creativity is actually *subnormative*: it manifests itself uniquely, that is, in the lateral and inappropriate paths that happen to open themselves to us just as we are forcing ourselves to conform to a determined norm. As paradoxical as it may seem, the state of exception has its original place of residence in an activity that is only seemingly obvious, which Wittgenstein calls "following a rule." This implies, inversely, that every humble application of a norm always contains within itself a fragment of the "state of exception." Jokes bring this fragment to light.

The second subordinate hypothesis sounds like this: the logical form of jokes consists of a deductive fallacy, or rather of an unmerited inference, or of an incorrect use of a semantic ambiguity. For example: attributing to the grammatical subject all the properties pertaining to its predicate; interchanging the part for the whole or the whole for the part; instituting a symmetrical relation between antecedent and consequent; treating a metalinguistic expression as though it were a language-object. In brief, it seems to me that there is an accurate and meticulous correspondence between the various types of wit catalogued by Freud and the paralogisms examined by Aristotle in his study *On Sophistical Refutations*. In the case of jokes, the deductive fallacies reveal, however, a productive nature: that is, they are used for making something; they are mechanisms that are indispensable for performing a verbal action that "bewilders and illuminates" (Freud, *Jokes*: 8). A delicate question arises here. In fact, if it is true that jokes are the diagram of innovative action, we will have to suppose that their logical form, or fallacy, plays an important role, since it has to do with changing the very mode of living. But is it not bizarre to structure the creativity of *Homo sapiens* around faulty reasoning, around error? Certainly it is: bizarre and worse. It would be foolish, however, to believe that anyone could be so silly as to support a hypothesis constructed in this manner. The truly interesting point here is to understand

under which circumstances and under which conditions the paralogism ceases to be ... a paralogism; or rather, to be *not* able to
be considered incorrect or false (in the rigorous logical sense, let
us be careful to note). It goes without saying that only under
these circumstances and under these conditions does the "fallacy"
become an indispensable resource of innovative action.

Section 1

How to Do New Things with Words

1

From the Third Person Intruder

to the Public Sphere

I do not intend to discuss Freud's theses on jokes, nor, far less, to criticize them. It is enough for me to show that a radically different explanation of these same phenomena is *also* legitimate. And that this alternate explanation takes root precisely in certain Freudian observations.

Jokes, for Freud, are "made" (Freud, *Jokes*: 224), as opposed to the comical situation, which must simply be traced down and recognized. Whoever coins a joke does something new: "*Have you taken a bath?*" someone asks severely of a very dirty friend. "*What, is there one missing?*" the friend replies, unperturbed (ibid: 55). Moreover, while the comical dimension can be completely, or only in part, nonlinguistic, the joke is exclusively verbal. Those who say something witty do something new; let us note carefully, something they could *not* have done without words. The retort alters the situation into which it enters, thanks to certain semantic and rhetorical prerogatives in its possession, as outlined by Freud right at the beginning of *Witz*: "the coupling of dissimilar things, contrasting ideas, 'sense in nonsense', the succession of bewilderment and enlightenment, the bringing forward of what is hidden, and the peculiar brevity of wit" (ibid: 11).

Doing something new with words: this general characteristic does not allow us, however, to grasp fully the nature of jokes. In and of itself, it does not clarify the situation sufficiently: even those who elaborate upon an ingenious metaphor create something new with words. On the other hand, the Freudian identikit of verbal creativity at work within the joke suggests, preliminarily, an affinity between "joke-work" and "dream-work": even the dreamer, in fact, proceeds by way of "the approach of dissimilar elements, the contrast of representation, the sense of the absurd." The distance that separates jokes from other forms of linguistic invention, but also and above all from the realm of dreams, is attested to even by Freud himself, when he emphasizes—on a number of occasions and in the most diverse contexts, as happens with every self-respecting *refrain*—the nullifying role played, *only* in the act of joke making, by the so-called "third person." What does this mean?

The first person, Freud says, is the author of the joke; the second is the object or the target of it; the third, ultimately, is its "audience," that is, the neutral spectator who evaluates the witty remark, understanding perfectly the meaning of the remark, and takes pleasure in it. The third person, superfluous or, worse yet, optional in the comical situation, is, instead a *necessary* component of the joke. Let us try to understand: the third person is not limited to amplifying the effects of the witticism; this "intruder" actually makes it possible. Without the spectator, jokes indeed would not exist. "No-one can be content with having made a joke for himself alone" (ibid: 175): in other words, a *private* or *interior* humorous remark is inconceivable. However, the presence of the interlocutor-victim is not in any way sufficient for mitigating this dissatisfaction. Freud considers every joke that remains confined within the sticky relationship between sender and receiver to be a shot in the dark.

The third person is a logical condition of the joke: the "I" and the "you" depend absolutely upon this third person. Without an audience, the actors would have no way of knowing exactly which script they have recited. Whoever produces the remark that abruptly modifies the trajectory of the dialogue does not succeed in laughing, or does so only upon reflection, thanks, that is, to the amusement of which the third person gives proof. This impediment to the direct enjoyment of one's own witticism, according to Freud, is owed to two distinct, and therefore, convergent reasons. The first is this: the author of the joke cannot judge whether it has hit its target or if it is, instead, akin to simple nonsense. The choice between sense and non-sense does not fall within the competence of the witticist (nor of the deuteragonist who has been ridiculed). So then, the disinterested spectator "has the decision passed over to him on whether the joke-work has succeeded in its task—as though the self did not feel certain in its judgment on the point" (ibid: 176). And here is the second reason for the impediment to laughter: the "tendentious" remark, consisting of aggressive or obscene content, and, equally, the "innocent" remark, that restores the childish habit of playing with words as though they were things, require of the person who coins the remark a conspicuous waste of psychic energy in order to overcome all sorts of inhibitions, "external or internal" (ibid: 181, fol.). For makers of jokes, the work entailed in making something new (and not agreed upon) erodes and neutralizes their eventual "profit of pleasure." The third person, on the other hand, who shares the same inhibitions as the joke teller, can enjoy the overcoming of these inhibitions without assuming any psychic waste: that is why the third person laughs heartily. This laughter, being exempt from counterbalancing, accomplishes the target of the remark.

Even while considering this "third person" to be so important, Freud assigns to this person the limited function of doing nothing more than signaling the characteristics for which the witticism is *absolutely* not reducible to dream-work: "A dream is a completely asocial mental product; it has nothing to communicate to anyone else. [....] A joke, on the other hand, is the most social of all the mental functions whose goal is pleasure. It often calls for three persons and its completion requires the participation of someone else in the mental process it starts" (ibid: 222). It seems to me, however, that one cannot overlook the contribution of the spectator to the success of the joke. This contribution, rather than being limited to disturbing or objecting to the joke = dream equation, actually offers the opportunity for formulating an equation which is totally different: *joke* = *praxis*. The figure of the third person as intruder, in addition to being outside the realm of dream-work, also demands, in the positive sense, the introduction of pertinent concepts that define appropriately the figure's importance. This "intruder" is a point of departure, not a left-over entity.

The condition of the third person clarifies the meaning of "doing something new with words" in the case of the joke. A "doing" whose reality depends entirely upon the presence of outsiders and, in the strongest and most complete sense, upon *public action*. It is nothing less, let us understand, than a political discourse held in a general assembly that urges towards insurrection against the constituent powers: if enunciated in the absence of witnesses, it is as though this discourse had never occurred. The intrinsic necessity of exposing oneself to the observation and judgment of one's equals carves out with precision the sphere of praxis. Within this sphere there are no gestures or utterances in possession of any autonomous significance. It is a sphere, that is, which can be separated from the world in which these gestures and utterances *appear* to the disinterested spectator (to the anonymous "s/he," let us note, and not to the "you" to whom the gesture or utterance is addressed). In order to invent a metaphor, indiscreet eyes are not necessary: the first two persons are sufficient, the speaking "I," and the "you" who is able to understand the innovative expression. On the other hand, those who utter a joke unexpectedly are in need of indiscreet eyes, because they are accomplishing an innovative action whose effective sense escapes, to a great degree, those who are directly implicated. The *praxis* can only occur by means of the "third person," for the same reasons which, according to Aristotle (See Aristotle, *Ethics*: 175–177) distinguish this third person from *epistéme* (pure knowledge) and from *poíesis* (production, doing). If the theoretical reflection eludes the observation of others and renders mute the world of appearances, praxis, instead, always presupposes and revives a public space. If production gives place to an independent object, or if it has an external goal, praxis, on the other hand, is an activity without a product, the result of which coincides entirely with its own performance. When action is consigned to exteriority and contingency (as opposed to *epistéme*), but deprived of an endurable product capable of certifying its reality (as opposed to *poíesis*), it can do nothing more than present itself again to the spectators. Its existence and its meaning are entrusted to the witness-judges.

In order to understand the strategic importance of the "third person" in the joke, there is no better strategy that to turn to the philosophy of Kant. The truly great event, for example, of the French Revolution of 1789, can only be understood by those who were "not themselves caught up in it," but who limited themselves to following it with a "*sympathy* that borders almost on enthusiasm," thus experiencing a form of "inactive delight" (Kant, "Contest": 182, fol.). The advantage of the spectator consists in intertwining the actions as a whole, while the actors (first and second person) know only their own parts. In her lectures on Kant's *Critique of Judgment*, Hannah Arendt observed that, for Kant, the spectator represents the only effective antidote to the weakness and opaqueness that distinguish praxis. Whoever witnessed the Revolution without taking part in it saw "what counted most; he could discover a meaning in the course taken by events, a meaning that the actors ignored; and the existential ground for his insight was his disinterestedness, his nonparticipation, his noninvolvement" (Arendt: 54). Let us remember the two reasons for the impediment to laughter for those who invent the joke for the purpose of producing laughter: on one hand, the author is not capable of evaluating whether the joke has succeeded or failed; on the other hand, the author's pleasure is curtailed by the work necessary for shaking the resistance of the status quo (or of the "inhibitions"). These same reasons hold also, on a completely different scale, for the protagonists of revolutions; even those revolutionaries who are deprived of a vision of the whole and overcome by the waste of energy, can enjoy their own feats only as a reflection, thanks to the assistance of the audience. "For the actor, the decisive question is thus how he appears to others [*dokei hois allois*]; the actor is dependent on the opinion of the spectator; he is not autonomous (in Kant's language); he does not conduct himself according to an innate voice of reason but in accordance with what spectators would expect of him. The standard is the spectator" (ibid: 55). With regard to the joke, but also to the political praxis discussed by Kant and Arendt, a misunderstanding is always possible: this misunderstanding consists in extenuating, and, in certain cases, in completely abolishing the distinction between second and third person. By doing so, one will be content with repeating some obvious certainties: there is no such thing as private language—nor is there the possibility of private praxis; the human mind is fundamentally social, etc. But here the essential point is lost: the difference between amorous dialogue, or scientific conversation, for which the second person is sufficient, and a joke, or a revolution, which need, instead, an indifferent audience in order to exist. In certain jokes (let us think of word "games" not directed to a particular interlocutor), the second person may be missing, the "you." In none of these jokes do we find the third person, the inactive and judging "s/he." To reduce the third person to the second, or to amalgamate them, means to misunderstand the specific statute of *praxis*, and also, to preclude the understanding of the joke. Arendt writes: "We [...] are inclined to think that in order to judge a spectacle you must first have the spectacle—that the spectator is secondary to the actor; we tend to forget that no one in his right mind would ever put on a spectacle without being sure of having spectators to watch it" (ibid: 61–62). This deplorable inclination affects today's philosophy of the mind.

The "third person" authorizes the interchangeability of the joke and *public action*. Furthermore, we know that this has to do with a *linguistic action*. Certainly there are analogies to be drawn between witty utterances and the performative utterances studied by Austin ("I baptize this baby Luca," "I declare the session open," etc.). In both cases: 1) an action is carried out with words, an action that could not have been carried out otherwise; 2) it is useless to attempt to reduce that which is *done* to the "thought content" of the phrases uttered; 3) these phrases, constituting an action in and of themselves, are not true or false—rather, they are successful or unsuccessful (fortunate or unfortunate, in Austin's terminology).

Nevertheless, even if we were to choose to neglect their considerable formal heterogeneity, the fact remains that the performative utterance is clearly distinguished from the witty remark by virtue of its stereotypical and repetitive character. Since this has to do with a semijuristic and customary formula (order, pardon, promise, etc.), the same utterance is valid for all analogous occasions. Vice versa, the joke provokes bewilderment and astonishment, and for this very reason it does not allow for reiterations: "the very nature of surprising someone or taking him unawares implies that it cannot succeed a second time" (Freud, *Jokes*: 188–189). Beyond the public and linguistic realms, the joke accomplishes an innovative action. In fact, as we shall see, it is this action that illustrates in a specialized manner the procedures and aptitudes that will be utilized, in general, by the most diverse *innovative actions*. The witty remark clearly recapitulates the techniques to which human praxis has recourse in a critical juncture, when the old compasses are knocked out of order by a magnetic storm: making wise use of nonsense and of absurd reasoning; making improper connections between distant thoughts; having recourse to semantic ambivalence in order to make a turn onto a side street; shifting the psychic accent on a theme different from the initial theme, and so on.

2

Witty Remarks and the Philosophy of Praxis

The "third person" casts a bridge between joke and praxis. If the bridge holds up, we will need to apply to jokes in their entirety— beginning with the production of each joke by the "first person"—many of the concepts pertaining specifically to praxis. The linguistic acts studied by Freud are, perhaps, suitable for comparison to some of the key-words that stand out in Aristotle's *Nicomachean Ethics*: a) *phrónesis*, or practical know-how; b) *orthós logos*, the discourse that enunciates the correct norm according to which the action in one single case takes shape; c) the perception of *kairós*, of the proper moment for performing an action; d) *éndoxa*, that is, the opinions prevalent from time to time within a community of speakers.

a) A successful joke bears witness, on the part of its creator, to the presence of a gift or an ability difficult to classify. As Freud himself notes, humor does not take root in strictly cognitive faculties, such as speculative intelligence, memory, imagination (See Freud, *Jokes*: 169–170). A public action, whose goal coincides absolutely with its execution, requires instead that type of keenness that Aristotle calls phrónesis (a slippery term which translators, for the most part, render pompously as "wisdom"). *Phrónesis* is the ability to evaluate the appropriate thing to do within a contingent circumstance. What distinguishes it from the other practical virtues (courage, impartiality, etc.) is the fact that it does not limit itself to choosing a behavior based upon a given norm; rather, it establishes which norm is appropriate to a concrete situation.

The particular situation, which both the *phrónimos* and the joke teller must confront, is always characterized by a high level of uncertainty: so much so that, according to Aristotle, it "cannot be attained by science but only by 'perception'" (Aristotle, *Ethics*: 182). But "it is useless to apply a definite yardstick to something indefinite" (ibid: 167). Thus, for the *phrónimos* and for the joke teller, the application of the rule is one and the same as the identification of the rule. Let us think of a war: the virtue of courage drives the soldier to fight with valor; but *aorístou kai kanón estin*, which "concerns that which is good or evil for man," manifests itself above all in the act of deciding if the clear principle to which the soldier should conform in a given situation is courage, or moderation, or reluctance to obey unjust orders, or some other principle. Let us think also, in a parallel manner, of a witty story dear to Freud. An impoverished gentleman obtains, as a loan, a small sum of money from an acquaintance. The next day, the benefactor meets the gentleman at a restaurant where he is seated in front of a plate of salmon with mayonnaise. He reprimands him resentfully: "'Is *that* what you've used my money for?' 'I don't understand you', replied the object of the attack; 'if I haven't any money I *can't* eat salmon mayonnaise, and if I have some money I *mustn't* eat salmon mayonnaise. Well, then, when *am* I to eat salmon mayonnaise?'" (Freud, *Jokes*: 56). The response of the penniless gourmet, "has been very markedly given the form of a logical argument" (ibid: 57); it succeeds in accomplishing a "shifting of the psychical emphasis" (ibid: 57). The shifting consists in applying/instituting, in reference to a particular situation, a (fortunate) norm that supplants the (ascetic) norm which the interlocutor draws upon automatically. This shifting is always possible when *aorístos kai kanón estin* is nothing other than the exercising of *phrónesis*. Here, humor consists of placing in evidence the contrast between a determined virtue (frugality) and the insight needed for evaluating which virtue is appropriate to a singular and unrepeatable event.

Phrónesis has its authentic testing ground in cases "which no law can be framed to cover and which can only be met by a special regulation" (Aristotle, *Ethics*: 167). In contrast to a law (*nómos*), a decree (*pséphisma*) concerns a circumscribed event which has limited duration in time. Aristotle compares the *pséphisma* to the "leaden rule" employed by the architects of Lesbos: "Just as that rule is flexible and can be bent to take the shape of the stone, so a special decree or regulation can be made to fit the particular conditions" (ibid: 167). The adaptability of the principle to the contingent situation, of the measuring device to the shape of the stone: this is the resource in which the shrewd person and the author of the joke place their trust. Only within the confines of a decree does the application of the norm coincide, without vestiges, with the institution: it is applied by the very act of instituting itself. Only in a decree does the "just mean" (*to méson*, the behavior appropriate to a specific circumstance), far from presupposing its own extremes (excess and defect), actually create them or make possible their definition. Every joke that hits its target has something of this *pséphisma* in it. A guy who happened to have met Rothschild is answering his friends who want to know all about the magnate: "he treated me quite as his equal—quite *famillionairely* [italics mine]" (ibid: 14). Like the decree, that word "famillionairely" is both the principle and the application of the principle: a platinum ruler which measures itself.

b) *Phrónesis*, Aristotle writes, is found when "the means are 'in accordance with the right principle' [*orthós logos*]" (Aristotle, *Ethics*: 171). What is it that makes up the *orthótes*, the correctness, of the *lógos* upon which practical shrewdness rests? We already know this: the discourse is clear when, and only when, it enunciates the appropriate norm for a particular situation. But what is guaranteed if the "correct discourse," the cornerstone of *phrónesis*, is truly correct? Nothing other than *phrónesis* itself, Aristotle replies. For anyone who has leafed through the *Nicomachean Ethics*, it is well known that between *phrónesis* and *orthós logos* a circular relationship is in force, since the two notions imply each other and support each other in turn. Insight exists on the condition that the appropriate norm is enunciated; but the appropriate norm exists on the condition that there is insight. This circularity, always experienced anew by the person who acts by speaking, is the mental equivalent of the *decree*: in both cases, the unit of measure is itself measured precisely by that which it measures. One could also say: the reciprocal dependence between *phrónesis* and *orthós logos* shows that the decree (in which it is impossible to distinguish the application of the norm from its institution) is not a cloudy, extreme case; rather, it is the base form of human praxis.

The joke is a public action that can be accomplished solely by means of words. And it is a peculiar exercise in *phrónesis*, in practical shrewdness. Let us now ask what role the "correct discourse" plays in all of this. In the case of the witty comment, the *orthós logos* is not limited to inspiring or guiding the innovative action; instead, it is an integral part of it. Put in other terms: it often happens that a joke achieves an action by means of the enunciation—indirect and sometimes sly, such that it "bewilders and illuminates"—of the norm appropriate to that action. An example: after having looked at the oil portraits of two *nouveau riche* scoundrels, an art critic points to the space between the two canvases and asks: "Where is the Saviour?" (*Freud*, Jokes: 87). The successful joke is *orthós logos*. But it is, we must note, an *orthós logos* whose metaoperative character (as is necessary) is completely absorbed at the operative level (i.e., the concrete features of the linguistic action one is executing). Furthermore, the witty remark is an *orthós logos* the utterance of which arouses *pleasure*. This aspect of the *orthós logos*, which can never be overlooked, raises an interesting problem. For Aristotle, the coupling of the pleasurable/painful also determines the behavior of non-linguistic animals: thus, the pursuit of pleasure does not depend, in and of itself, on a "correct discourse." The *orthós logos* is concerned, above all, with the couplings of useful/harmful and just/unjust (Aristotle, *Politics*: 60). What is it that happens, then, in the joke? The linguistic principle, which usually permits us to discriminate between the life of good and the life of evil, becomes here the primary material and the instrument for playful experimentation. We play with the *orthós logos*. It is quite true that in the praxis of the human animal verbal reasoning ends up regulating even the pursuit of pleasure (see Lo Piparo: 19–20). But the joke presents a curious anomaly: in the joke, the *orthós logos*, rather than governing pleasure, becomes the *immediate object* of pleasure.

c) *Phrónesis* in general, and the inclination for inventing surprising witty comments in particular, requires the ability to have a good eye and quick reflexes. A good eye: practical shrewdness, as opposed to the single virtue which adheres always to a specific situation, consists precisely of the ability to weigh and evaluate the most diverse situations. Quick reflexes: those who act within the public sphere must grasp the proper moment (*kairós*) in order to make their moves. The witty remark fails if it is not made at the right moment. "Serenissimus was making a tour through his provinces and noticed a man in the crowd who bore a striking resemblance to his own exalted person. He beckoned to him and asked: '*Was your mother at one time in service in the Palace?*'—'No, your Highness,' was the reply, '*but my father was*'" (Freud, *Jokes*: 79–80). One moment earlier would have been too early and one moment later too late. The *phrónimos* joke teller singles out, from inside the verbal plot, the temporal spiral that from time to time is inserted into the plot and which alone can render the joke congruent. And the joke teller does not allow it to escape. "An innkeeper had a whitlow on his finger and the baker said to him: '*You must have got that by putting your finger in your beer.*' 'It wasn't that', replied the innkeeper, '*I got a piece of your bread under my nail*'" (ibid: 79). Seizing the *kairós*, the opportune moment, is the condition that renders the humorous utterance effective, or even, simply, sensible (that is to say, understandable). The innovative action is an urgent action, accomplished under the pressure of unrepeatable circumstances. Those who accomplish it are always in a state of emergency.

Freud writes: "We speak [....] of 'making' a joke, but we are aware that when we do so our behaviour is different from what it is when we make a judgement or make an objection. A joke has quite outstandingly the characteristic of being a notion that has occurred to us 'involuntarily'" (ibid: 207). It is quite true that people behave in a different way: the explanation lies, however, in the fact that the inventor of the joke, not someone who pronounces a judgment or makes an objection, accomplishes a *public action* (the outcome of which is entrusted to the "third person"). The difference pointed out by Freud is, approximately, that which separates *praxis* from *epistéme*. What remains to be understood, nevertheless, is the reason for which the joke presents itself as an "involuntary 'idea'." Is it necessary here to make reference to dream-work? I do not think so. To recognize the *kairós* and to take advantage of it requires quick reflexes. Without this necessary promptness, the innovative action fails and the joke collapses into an enigmatic and irrational voice. Thus, the "joking allusion" appears, "without my being able to follow these preparatory stages in my thoughts" (ibid: 208). In the presence of a critical situation, *phrónesis* takes on the appearance of a *semiinstinctive reaction*. And the joke does the same. We will need to return to this semi-instinctive reaction later (in Chapter 4 of this study). It is enough to observe, for now, that this reaction enters again, and rightly so, into the sphere of praxis, given that it coincides with the appreciation of the *kairós* and the elaboration of behavior in accordance with a state of exception. Let us quote Freud once again: "What happens is not that we know a moment beforehand what joke we are going to make, and that all it then needs is to be clothed in words" (ibid: 207). Precisely. But this observation holds not only for the joke: strictly speaking, it *never* occurs that there is an already constituted thought that afterwards will be embellished by words. The joke, precisely because it is motivated by the necessity of seizing the moment, exhibits with exemplary precision that which is always true: the integrally *verbal* character of human thought. The fact that we think with words becomes empirically evident (I will know what I was thinking only after having said it!) when the process of thinking-speaking executes an innovative action, an action that, in order to accomplish its goal, must take place *precisely now*.

d) In a manner similar to that of *phrónesis* and of rhetorical discourse intended to persuade, the joke also has as its background the *éndoxa*, that is, the opinions and beliefs shared by a community. The *éndoxa* are not facts; they are linguistic customs. More precisely, they are linguistic customs so embedded as to constitute the implicit presupposition of every type of reasoning. In the terminology of Wittgenstein, one can say that the *éndoxa* (or at least their core, consisting of collective convictions that are almost unquestionable) are the *grammar* of a form of life. These shared beliefs have to do with "such things as are in a way common for all to grasp and belong to no delimited science" (Aristotle, *Rhetoric*: 66). The joke utilizes, by handfuls, the *éndoxa*: with the goal, however, of corroding them from within. Its point of honor lies in illustrating the questionable nature of the opinions lying beneath discourses and actions. In order to hit its target, the joke pushes one single belief to the limit, to the point of extracting absurd and ridiculous consequences from it. Or it maliciously places in contrast two fundamental principles, each of which, if considered separately, seemed incontrovertible. The joke is a rhetorical syllogism that refutes the same *éndoxa* from which it got its start. Or, better yet: it is a performative example of how the grammar of a form of life can be transformed.

In the joke, the *éndoxa* serve as "inhibitions" to be overcome. Let us recall once again the hypothesis proposed by Freud: those who coin a joke cannot laugh at it (until after the "third person" has laughed at it) because of the enormous psychic waste it has cost them to break with tenacious prohibitions. These prohibitions are nothing more than the peculiar way in which the principles and beliefs that form the background for social communication make themselves evident. They are nothing other than *éndoxa*. According to Freud, the inhibitions-*éndoxa*, for the most part, have to do with homage to the hierarchy and respect for sexual decorum. But they have to do also with exercising the faculty of language: a ban has been placed, in fact, on the infantile tendency to engage in the use of homophones and alliterations in order to obtain inappropriate and surprising semantic strings of words. The joke functions only if the inhibitions, which the author of the joke seeks to overcome, are rooted also in the passive spectator. Were this not so, the "third person" could not gain any pleasure from overcoming the inhibitions. "Laughing at the same jokes is evidence of far-reaching psychical conformity" (Freud, *Jokes*: 185). This conformity is further assured by the *éndoxa*: even when this occurs in a purely negative way, as the target of criticism and the object of confutation, the *éndoxa* do not cease to unite the speakers. Inhibitions aside, there are many other linguistic customs linking joke tellers to their audiences: stereotypes, proverbs, rules, idiomatic expressions, traditional anecdotes. The witty action takes advantage of their notoriety, but only in order to maim them and to overturn their meaning. In commenting on the resignation of a stupid government minister, a journalist observes: "Like Cincinnatus, he has gone back to his place before the plough" (ibid: 27). And then: a very reserved gentleman, after having been pestered for while by a petulant chatterbox, reports the situation in this way: "I drove with him *tête à bête*" (ibid: 25).

The persuasive discourse takes its "reasons from generally accepted opinions [*éndoxa*]" (Aristotle, *Topica*: 273). The joke, as has been noted, disrupts and delays the same *éndoxa* from which it takes its form; or, at least, it extracts from the *éndoxa* consequences so bizarre as to cause it to retroact, like a hammer, upon the very premises of the joke. Moreover, the persuasive discourse and the joke are comparable because both are characterized by an intrinsic *conciseness*. We understand that the rhetorical syllogism, the enthymeme, is essentially full of gaps, such that it omits a premise or even the conclusion: far from being a defect, brevity allows for "leveraging what is not said, so as to share with the interlocutor the responsibility of the thought process" (Piazza: 146). The same holds true, to a certain degree, for the joke, although one might add that the joke aims at sharing with the "third person" (*not* with the direct interlocutor) the grave responsibility of refuting the *éndoxa*. But something must be added to the specific conciseness of the joke.

Freud quotes, with approval, a phrase from Theodor Lipps: "A joke says what it has to say, not always in few words, but in *too* few words—that is, in words that are insufficient by strict logic or by common modes of thought and speech" (Freud, *Jokes*: 11). After having suggested the idea that the author of the joke would favor the abbreviated expression in order to enjoy certain psychic "savings," Freud himself admits that this explanation does not hold true: choosing the correct word (for example, the adverb "famillionairely," with regard to the Rothschild example previously noted), the word capable of uniting, in and of itself, two contrasting thoughts, implies at least as much effort as the process of reasoning in complete detail. The savings accomplished by the witty technique "remind us, perhaps, of the way in which some housewives economize when they spend time and money on a journey to a distant market because vegetables are to be had there a few farthings cheaper" (ibid: 48). Once the hypothesis of the "savings" has been discarded, let us ask ourselves what is the reason for the notion that the joke is concise in and of itself, even when it is elongated into a thousand details, omitting nothing. It seems to me that this notion is closely connected to the innovative character of the witty action; or to the fact that the notion breaks away abruptly from the prevailing *éndoxa* and offers a glimpse of other *éndoxa* by way of a decree (*pséphisma*) promulgated in due time (*kairós*). The words that a joke utilizes seem *always* insufficient, precisely because they diverge from the "communal ways of thinking and speaking." The joke opens up an oblique path that links together heterogeneous semantic contents previously unrelated. This path, that is to say, the inventive inference, seems short because it did not exist before (nor was it foreseen), and not because there was another longer path available. Every linguistic action that modifies the grammar of a form of life is certainly concise: but here we speak of an *absolute conciseness*, not of a comparative one.

Human praxis sets up camp within the environment of the contingent. It is focused, then, on "variable subject matter [*to endechómenon állos échein*]" (Aristotle, *Ethics*: 177). The joke, in its role as a diagram of innovative action, is not limited to actually operating within contingent situations; rather, it posits explicitly the theme of the contingence of all situations (and of the same *éndoxa* which prescribe the way in which these situations are to be dealt with). To put it in other terms: the joke illustrates clearly which aspect would be assumed by "variable subject matter," *if that subject matter were indeed variable*.

Section 2

Decision, Norm, Normality

The Leaky Kettle: Concerning the Difficulty

of Applying a Rule

The inconspicuous laboratory of the transformation of a form of life lies within the dissimilar, and at times, contradictory ways, in which it is possible to apply a rule to a particular case. The "creativity" of the human animal is nothing other than a response to the dilemmas provoked by this application. Jokes exhibit the logicolinguistic resources that nurture innovation in general, precisely because they are found in a no-man's land that separates any norm from its own realization within a contingent situation. The joke is the loquacious sentry of this no-man's land: it shows, again and again, how tortured, and subject to abrupt diversions, is its own path.

How to apply a rule to a particular case: the problem crops up again, in forms not all that different, in the *Nicomachean Ethics* of Aristotle, in Kant's *Critique of Judgement*, and in the *Philosophical Investigations* of Wittgenstein. We have just seen that for Aristotle, *phrónesis*, the practical know-how, has the job of choosing the virtue-rule that best fits a specific circumstance. Applying the norm is not so different from singling it out (or from instituting it, as happens in a decree). One could also say: the skill necessary to apply the rule is the *same* skill which, in another way, allows us to perceive which rule it is best to adopt in the present situation. This two-fold skill is, precisely, *phrónesis*. It seems to me that the amphibian character of *phrónesis* supports the thesis I shall try to justify extensively a little further on, after having laid down some new paths for my argument. It sounds somewhat like this: to apply a norm to a contingent situation always implies that we return, for a moment, *to this side of* the norm. And, vice versa: the only way to return truly to this side of the norm is to *apply it* to a contingent situation. With regard to Kant, it is enough to remember one of his declarations of principle in which he points out that no rule creates, at one and the same time, all the necessary and sufficient conditions for the subsumption of the particular case that lies beneath the rule (see also Garroni: 72–95). That is to say: no norm can indicate the modalities of its own concrete execution. With regard to Wittgenstein, it is to him that the next few pages will be dedicated. The sections of the *Philosophical Investigations* in which the author discusses what should be understood by "following a rule" offer the starting point for clarifying the structure of jokes, and *even*, the structure of innovative action.

"I said that the application of a word is not everywhere bounded by rules." This affirmation by Wittgenstein (Wittgenstein, *Investigations*: 33) means, certainly, that there are aspects of a linguistic game that are completely unregulated (just as, in tennis, there is no fixed height to which the ball must be sent at the moment of a hit); but it also means, and more radically, that a single movement of the game is never deducible from the rule of which that movement is also the application. The independence (or non-limitation) of the moment in which the rule is applied emerges in full in the presence of the corresponding rule, and not where the rule is missing. Between a norm and its effective realization there exists a lasting hiatus, indeed a real and true *incommensurability*.

The same incommensurability, to be clear, that distinguishes the relationship between the length of a circumference, and that of its diameter. It is known that there is no answer whatsoever to the calculation of that relationship, ending with the ellipses that stand for "and so on" (one is reminded of the Greek *pi*: 3.141592...). The same is true in our case. In fact, just a few lines after the affirmation by Wittgenstein cited above, he shows how inconclusive it is to claim to devise a rule by "determining the application of a rule" (ibid: 34): it is most obvious that this second rule, needing to be applied in its own turn, asks again for a third rule (which indicates how to apply the rule that determines the application of the rules); and so it continues, without stopping, as is typical of the regression to infinity.

The logical break between a norm and its realization within a particular difficult situation is illustrated in Section 85 of the *Philosophical Investigations*: "A rule stands there like a sign-post.—Does the sign-post leave no doubt open about the way I have to go? Does it show which direction I am to take when I have passed it; whether along the road or the footpath or cross-country? But where is it said which way I am to follow it; whether in the direction of its finger or (e.g.) in the opposite one?—And if there were not just a single sign-post, but a chain of adjacent ones or of chalk marks on the ground [*as if the rules were multiplying like crazy with the goal of guaranteeing one unambiguous application* (italics mine)]—is there only *one* way of interpreting them?" (ibid: 34). Well then, the uncertainty that reveals itself here with regard to the street sign is the fulcrum of *all* jokes. In the background of every joke lies the question with which Wittgenstein recapitulates the query: "But how can a rule show me what I have to do at *this* point?" (ibid: 68). Every joke puts into focus, in its own way, the variety of alternatives that come forth in applying a norm: rather than "continuing along the road" it is always possible "to take a side path, or go across the fields." But to take a side path, or to enter the fields, means to complete an innovative action: human "creativity" consists precisely and only in these digressions applied in the moment.

Double meaning, contradiction, multiple use of the same material, word games based on homophony, semantic shuffling brought on by eccentric inference: it is sufficient to list, topsy-turvy, the different techniques of humor studied by Freud in order to realize that each of these, without exception, highlights the *aporia* and the insistent paradoxes in the relationship between rule and application. Here is a *Witz* (joke) that could appropriately show up as the twin brother of Section 85 of the *Philosophical Investigations* (just substitute, for the road sign, the rule "it is necessary to justify oneself for one's own mistakes"): "A. borrowed a copper kettle from B. and after he had returned it was sued by B. because the kettle now had a big hole in it which made it unusable. His defense was: '*First, I never borrowed a kettle from B. at all; secondly, the kettle had a hole in it already when I got it from him; and thirdly, I gave him back the kettle undamaged* [italics mine]'" (Freud: 72). But, I repeat, there is not one joke, among those collected by Freud, that does not strike the same note. Let us consider a scurrilous double meaning: "Mr. and Mrs. X live in fairly grand style. Some people think that the husband has earned a lot and so has been able to lay by a bit [*sich etwas zurückgelegt*]; others again think that the wife has lain back a bit [*sich etwas zurückgelegt*] and so has been able to earn a lot" (ibid: 35). What else could this joke be, if not a stellar example of the Wittgensteinian principle according to which "the application of a word is not everywhere bounded by rules?" To avoid any misunderstandings, it is good to state precisely, at this point, that wit (*arguzia*) is not only an eccentric application (even if not an illegitimate one) of the rule. It is, rather, a concentrated display of the *relationship*, always problematic, because of its incommensurability, between the sphere of the norm and the sphere of actions, *quaestio iuris* e *quaestio facti*. One could say: the joke is the specific application of the rule which consists in emphasizing the constitutive difference between rule and application. But that would still be saying too little. As we shall see, shortly, the joke, just like the innovative action of which it is the diagram, applies a rule in an unusual fashion because—in the application of the rule, in order to apply it—it returns for a moment to that acumen, or sense of orientation, that *precedes* the rules and makes of them a formulation.

In the actual experience of talking, the road sign is language as a *system of signs*, while the different ways in which one can behave in the presence of these signs has to do with a *universe of discourse* language (that is, with "the activity of the speaker who puts language into action" (Benveniste: 256 [Note: English rendering, from the Italian edition, by the translators]). The distinction between the *semiotic* plane (sign) and the *semantic* plane (discourse), developed by Émile Benveniste in essays that form a watershed in the study of linguistics in the 20th century, corresponds in many ways to the distinction between the normative plane and the applicative plane. The semiotic system "exists in and of itself; it establishes the reality of language, but it does not require particular applications; the sentence, instead, the semantic expression, is *solely* particular" (ibid: 256). The sentence is not a "habitual event"; rather, it is a unique, "evanescent" event: in the sentence, "every word conserves only a little part of the value that it has in its role as sign" (ibid: 260). Under a semiotic profile, the contingent circumstances do not hold any weight; under the semantic profile, they are, however, decisive in providing meaning. In sum, what counts most is that "from the sign to the sentence there is no transition [...] they are separated by a hiatus" (ibid: 82). This is the same hiatus that always exists between the road sign and the ensuing actions it produces. The impossibility of deducing the *sense* of the discourse from the *meaning* of the signs, demonstrated in detail by Benveniste, is equivalent in every way to the impossibility of deducing from one certain rule that which must be its application in a specific situation. The joke is a discourse—particular, unique, evanescent—that gives a reckoning of the difference between the semiotic system and the universe of discourse. The comic effect derives, often, exactly from that coming and going between the two planes: inside one sentence one can see the diversity of the statute of the very same lexical entity, depending on whether it is interpreted as a sign, or as part of the discourse ("How's it going?" asks the blind man of the lame man; "Just as you see," the latter answers). Benveniste writes: "The privilege of language is that it can imply, at the same time, the significance of signs and the significance of utterance. This is where its greatest power lies, that of creating a second level of utterance in which it becomes possible to hold significant discourses about significance." (ibid: 81). Therefore, the joke is a peculiar case of significant discourse about significance. Peculiar for two reasons. First of all, because its metalinguistic content competes in executing a public action: the "second level of utterance" has, here, an immediate performative value. And secondly, because the joke is a meaningful discourse about the *crisis* of signification, given that it boldly emphasizes, with impudence, the independence of the application from the norm, that is, the unbridgeable distance between semantic and semiotic.

4

"The Common Behavior of Humankind"

and the State of Exception

Let us return to Wittgenstein. "This was our paradox: no course
of action could be determined by a rule, because any course of
action can be made out to accord with the rule. The answer was:
if *any* action can be made out to accord with the rule, then it can
also be made out to conflict with it. And so there would be neither
accord nor conflict here." (Wittgenstein, *Investigations*: 69). The
particular action does not agree with the rule, but neither does it
contradict the rule, because between one and the other there are
no points of contact, nor is there a common unit of measurement. In a manner of speaking, all logical friction is lacking. The
application of the norm consists in a *decision*; and the decision is
an event that cannot be likened to the norm, it is heterogeneous
to the norm. A negative relationship is in force between norm
and decision. To decide (from the word *caedere*, "to cut") means,
in fact, to *truncate* the regression to the infinite, to which is condemned every attempt to build the application of the rule in
question upon the structure of a further rule. The natural history
of the human animal is marked essentially by two phenomena,
both rooted in verbal language: the regression to the infinite,
whose appearances change according to the environments in which
it flourishes; and the possibility of interrupting this regression, a

possibility that branches out in a variety of forms and techniques. The decision is indeed the specific manner in which *praxis* halts the return to the infinite which is ingrained in the norms. It is the resource that permits those who act within the public sphere to place in opposition to one another the decisive "that's enough, that's it" and "so on and so forth," generated from the incommensurability between rule and application. Jokes give first hand information on how the resource-decision works.

Wittgenstein claims that "to follow a rule" is a collective habit: in front of a street sign I behave a certain way and not otherwise by virtue of an "established use," achieved through training and repetition. But what can be made of the decision, if everything depends on habit and on training? Does not the equation "to apply = to decide" clash against this authoritative Wittgensteinian assertion: "Following a rule is analogous to obeying an order"? (ibid: 70). The apparent difficulty arises from a mistaken understanding of the term "decision". This is a term that is surrounded, who knows why, by an aristocratic aura, almost such that "to truncate" (or "to cut away") is an activity reserved for those who exercise, in solitude, the mythological faculty of free will. Nothing could be more mistaken. "To truncate" (or "to cut away") is, rather, an opaque *biological necessity* for a living species whose operating rules (be they innate or acquired) do not contain within themselves any applicative criterion worthy of this name. The decision is the humble distinctive sign of a primate who has to deal (and here Gehlen is not wrong) with an over-abundance of drives that do not lend themselves to being translated into unambiguous behaviors. As soon as it is brought back to its literal significance, it is easy to realize that the word "decision" does not jar; rather, it falls into rhyming couplets with "habit," "repetition," and "obedience to an order." Habit, repetition, and obedience are all methods of *truncating* the experimental uncertainty when it is necessary to act in relation with a rule; they are all methods of *cutting away* the spider web of fictitious connections between the norm and its realization in a particular case; they are all methods of *deciding*. It follows that the applicative decision consists at times of disobeying the rule, by unusual behavior, or by surprising deflection. However, in these cases, to decide does not mean to show off free will, or to reveal "intentions" that are harbored deep inside, like eggs in a hidden nest. To follow a rule in bizarre and unexpected ways, even to ignore it, is still always public praxis: nothing that can be carried out alone, *privatim* (ibid: 69). To be exact, it is public praxis that prevails when a form of life implodes or crumbles, such as when a *crisis* occurs. It is precisely then, in fact, that the application of the norm demonstrates once again, and with maximum clarity, its *intrinsic* (that is, original and inevitable) problematic nature (as will be discussed in Chapter Seven). In front of the street sign, instead of reacting automatically by continuing straight ahead, one remains perplexed and might even turn off down a side street. But it is precisely this disturbing option, perfectly exemplified by jokes, which reveals that even the automatic continuing down the road was, for all intents and purposes, a *decision*.

Gloss: Wittgenstein and Schmitt

Wittgenstein's observations on that trite mystery that is the application of a rule to the particular case overlap, in many crucial aspects, with great juristic, decision-making thought. I limit myself here to a few stenographic notes, warning however, that the theme is deserving of being treated on its own merit.

In his *Political Theology*, Carl Schmitt, the authentic epicenter of 20th century tellurian philosophy of law, sets up a boundless polemic against Hans Kelsen's theory, according to which, "the basis for the validity of a norm can only be a norm [preliminary or additional, nevertheless different from the one in question]" [bracketed commentary mine] (Schmitt, *Theology*:19). A complete lack of legal and anthropological realism is necessary in order to believe that the operating "validity" of a rule is guaranteed by another rule, capable of providing the correct interpretation of the previous rule. Here we are facing the same question raised by Wittgenstein when he maintains "that the application of a word is not everywhere bounded by rules." It is indeed Wittgenstein, after all, who makes fun of the "Kelsenian" faith in the powers of *interpretation*. In Section 201 of his *Philosophical Investigations*, he notes that interpretation, being "the substitution of one expression of the rule for another" (Wittgenstein, *Investigations*: 69), gives rise to a false movement: "we give one interpretation after another; as if each one contented us at least for a moment, until we thought of yet another standing behind it" (ibid: 69). These are words that serve as counterpoint to Schmitt's sarcastic consideration: when one goes for an exact application of the norm, the hermeneutic illusion evaporates in a hurry, or at least it "existed ... only in that short interim period in which it was possible to answer the question 'Christ or Barabbas?' with a proposal to adjourn or appoint a commission of investigation" (Schmitt, *Theology*: 62).

From Schmitt's point of view, Kelsen's fault (and the fault of all those who reduce the State to a mere "production of laws") lies in having shamelessly ignored "the independent problem of the realization of the law" (ibid: 21). The application of the norm ignores the norm, requiring, rather, a *decision*. Between the "contents of the legal idea" and its effective execution, there lies a chronic dissonance (and sometimes an open contrast): "Every concrete juristic decision contains a moment of indifference from the perspective of content, because the juristic deduction is not traceable in the last detail to its premises" (ibid: 30). If examined from the point of view of the rule, the application "is, from the perspective of the content of the underlying norm, new and alien. Looked at normatively, the decision emanates from nothingness" (ibid: 31–32). But, this "nothingness" from which the decision would seem to arise, seems so only to those who accord an absolute primacy to the contents of the norm: it is enough to recognize the autonomy of the applicative moment to realize that the so called "nothingness" is, in reality, overflowing with behaviors and practices that are so basic as to characterize the very life of our species. As we shall soon see, both Schmitt and Wittgenstein place the decision within a normative void, yet one that is, at the same time, an anthropological fullness.

An inappropriate realization of the rule throws light, according to Schmitt, on the habitual realization of the rule. Even the most bizarre and transgressive applicative decision has its certain "juristic force", if only because, by modifying the real situation, it solicits the correction, or indeed the substitution, of the corresponding norm. But upon what foundation does the juristic force of a transgressive decision rest? Schmitt writes: "A logically consistent normativism must lead to the absurdity that the appropriate normative decision derives its force of law from the norm, whereas the norm-contradicting decision derives its force only out of itself, out of its norm-contradiction!" (Schmitt, *Juristic Thought*: 59–60). To avoid this game of three-card monte, one must, rather, conclude that the applicative decision does not *ever* obtain its peculiar juristic force from the rule. *Nor* does it seem to contradict the rule; *nor* does it seem to agree with the rule. To say it in Wittgenstein's words: "here neither agreement nor contradiction exists." The juristic force of the different reactions that can occur in front of the street sign, springs *only* from the fact that these reactions are all decisions (the automatic and thoughtless reaction no less than the innovative one). And the decision, like an Aristotelian decree, is a unit of measurement in and of itself.

For Schmitt, the antithesis between norm and decision touches upon "old theological and metaphysical problems, especially the question of whether God commands something because it is good or whether something is good because God commands it" (ibid: 59). The whole decisionist tradition—in sum, Schmitt's family album: Hobbes, de Maistre, Bonald, Donoso, Cortés—has unwaveringly supported the second alternative. God's command is a kind of pure "application" that, far from predicting the positive norm, anticipates it. One could say: in the beginning, there was the application; only afterwards did the rule come. "*Neque enim quia bonum est, idcirco auscultare debemus, sed quia deus praecepit.*" We must obey, not because it is about goodness, but because it is God who commands it. Tertullian's affirmation brings to its apex the independence of the executive decision with respect to the juristic-moral content of the norms. Wittgenstein has never moved away from this apex. One time it occurred to him to observe: "Schlick says that in theological ethics there used to be two conceptions of the essence of the good: according to the shallower interpretation the good is good because it is what God wants; according to the profounder interpretation God wants the good because it is good. I think that the first interpretation is the profounder one: *what God commands, that is good.* For it cuts off the way to any explanation 'why' it is good, while the second interpretation is the shallow, rationalist one, which proceeds 'as if' you could give reasons for what is good [italics mine]" (Waismann: 115). To believe that these words are the account of private nagging thoughts, having nothing to do with the study of linguistic games, means renouncing the understanding of an essential aspect of Wittgenstein's thinking. All the worse for those (Kripke, for example) who have lightheartedly abandoned this issue.

Schmitt holds that the "realization of the law," *that is, the decision,* is a prerogative exclusive to the state sovereignty. Wittgenstein holds that the always problematic application of the rule, *that is to say, the decision,* is the prerogative of every linguistic animal. Thus, the distinction does not occur between decisionism and normativism, but between two dissimilar forms of decisionism: the first, monopolistic; the second, diffuse (indeed inevitably, because it is ingrained in the very nature of verbal language). And it cannot by any means be said that the applications/decisions of the speakers may not rebound against the applications/decisions of the sovereigns. "On the other hand a language/game does change with time," writes Wittgenstein (Wittgenstein, *Certainty*: 34–E).

"Following a rule" has its moment of truth in the critical situation in which different applications of the same norm proliferate, irreconcilable between themselves. This is the state of exception of linguistic praxis. But it is also, at the same time, the official residence of *Witz*. Wittgenstein carefully describes the critical situation in Section 206 of the *Philosophical Investigations*. "*Following a rule* is analogous to obeying an order. We are trained to do so; we react to an order in a particular way. But what if one person reacts *in one way* and another *in another* to the order and the training? Which one is right? [italics mine]" (Wittgenstein, *Investigations*: 70). The plurality of heterogeneous applications is no longer, in this case, a theoretical eventuality (as in the case of the traffic light); rather, it is the effective reality (a reality well depicted in the joke about the leaky kettle). Nor can we appeal to training or to habit: these devices, which earlier allowed us to *get rid* of doubts and controversies, now spin about aimlessly; they are part of the problem, certainly not part of the solution. Well then, what happens when the thorny fact that "my actions" have nothing to do with the "expression of the rule" becomes completely apparent (ibid: 68)? How can one articulate human praxis in the state of exception? To answer this question is not so different from clarifying, once and for all, the *modus operandi* of the joke.

To apply a rule in so many different ways means suspending it, placing it provisionally outside of the game. From the cognitive point of view, it is as if one were to ignore it. There are many and varied applications, but it would be hard to say precisely to which rule they belong. To visualize the suspension/ignorance of the norm, Wittgenstein falls back on an ethnological example. Section 206 continues as follows: "Suppose you came as an explorer into an unknown country with a language quite strange to you. In what circumstances would you say that the people there gave orders, understood them, obeyed them, rebelled against them, and so on? *The common behavior of mankind is the system of reference* by means of which we interpret an unknown language [italics mine]" (ibid: 70). The critical situation is compared to listening to a language one has never heard before. In order to best orient ourselves in front of the quick progression of incomprehensible sounds (if you will: of applications that apparently do not correspond to any rules), we can count on one criterion: "the common behavior of mankind," *die gemeinsame menschliche Handlungsweise.* Here is the nullifying notion. What is it about? In question are the distinctive traits of our species, the fundamental (that is, the inevitable) dispositions of the linguistic animal. It is legitimate to suppose that "the common behavior of mankind" coincides to a large degree with the "natural history" of which Wittgenstein speaks, almost at the beginning of the *Philosophical Investigations*, in Section 25: "Commanding, questioning, storytelling, chatting [but also, from § 23, forming and testing a hypothesis, guessing riddles, making a joke; telling it, thanking, cursing, greeting, praying] are as much a part of our natural history as walking, eating, drinking, playing" (ibid: 10–11). The Wittgensteinian explorer, and those who act within a critical situation, come back *to this side of* the rule (the latter being unknown or suspended) and adopt as a "reference system" a set of vital species-specific behaviors. Such behaviors are the "bedrock" underlying all the norms determined by content. On this side of the rules there exists a basic *regularity*. The critical situation makes this *regularity* visible; it pushes it forward to center stage; it makes it occupy the entire stage.

Also for the juristic theory, the state of exception, far from resembling an unformed void, is the occasion in which the essential web of human life earns an unexpected importance. Or better: it is the occasion in which the warp of human life gains unexpected prominence. The suspension of the *norm* permits the surfacing of the *normality* of practices, customs, relationships, inclinations, conflicts. According to Carl Schmitt, "Because the exception is different from anarchy and chaos, order in the juristic sense still prevails even if it is not of the ordinary kind" (Schmitt, *Theology*: 12). This nonjuristic order, that is, "the common behavior of mankind," is characterized by a radical blurring of fields and contexts, given that, in this case, there is no other rule but the application. In Wittgenstein's terms, one could say: The state of exception cancels the border between grammatical clauses and empirical clauses; it makes it impossible to discern the riverbed from the river's waters that flow within it. Schmitt writes: "The exception appears in its absolute form when a situation in which legal prescriptions can be valid must first be brought about. Every general norm demands *a normal, everyday frame of life* to which it can be factually applied and which is subjected to its regulations. The norm requires a homogeneous medium. This effective normal situation is not a mere 'superficial presupposition' that a jurist can ignore; that situation belongs precisely to its immanent validity [italics mine]" (ibid: 13). The state of exception poses the problem, once again, of connecting *regularity*—"a normal everyday frame of life"—to a *rule*: eventually to a completely unpublished rule, or, at any rate, to one that is considerably different from that which was previously in force.

Looked at closely, any application of a norm whatsoever requires us to reflect upon the anthropological backdrop that Wittgenstein calls "the common behavior of mankind." The permanent rift between the content of the norm and its realization is surpassed by seeking again, always, the field that preceded the norms and that renders their definition possible. Thus three, not only two, are the levels upon which action is articulated: a) regularity or "the common behavior of mankind"; b) the determined rule; c) the contingent application of the determined rule. The application, never inferable from the corresponding rule, aligns itself, to a certain extent, with regularity. The positive side of the decision lies here (the therapeutic-negative side, as we know, consists of the interruption of the return to the infinite): "to cut away" means building a short circuit between that which comes after the rule (application) and that which comes before it (regularity). The applicative decision returns to the "normal everyday frame of life" and, moving from there, selects, from the start, the norm to be followed. This is not so different from the double skill that makes up *phrónesis*. Now, if it is true that the reference to "the common behavior of mankind" is present, even if in veiled form, in *every* application of a rule to a particular case, one must also conclude that a fragment of the state of exception is wedged into *every* application of a rule. There is always a moment, in the concrete realization of a norm, in which one returns *to the other side* of the norm.

This does not lessen, however, the difference between the routine and the critical situation. If one makes use of parentheses in order to indicate a term that, without a doubt, has a role to play, even if it remains in the background, then routine could be schematically rendered in this fashion: ("normal everyday frame of life")—positive norm—execution. The critical situation is rendered, instead, like this: "normal everyday frame of life"—(positive norm)—execution. Only the state of exception correctly stated—"what if one person reacts in one way and another in another?" (Wittgenstein, *Investigations*: 70)—suspends or deprives of authority a set *rule* in the name of species-specific *regularity*. Only the state of exception suspends the usual distinction between grammatical clauses and empirical clauses, setting up a hybrid region—since hybrid is, in and of itself, regularity: grammatical but also empirical, empirical but also grammatical. Only the state of exception emphasizes without reservation the autonomy of the applicative moment, to the point of delineating a virtuous circle between it and "the common behavior of mankind." Only the state of exception determines an upheaval of perspective, by virtue of which *the rule must be considered a particular case of the application.*

We find innovation, "the displacement of the psychic accent," the abrupt deviation from the paths followed until now, when and only when, in applying a certain norm, we are obliged to sneak up behind that norm and to call upon "the common behavior of humankind." Strange as it may seem, the creativity of the linguistic animal is triggered by a *return*: by the intermittent return, demanded by a critical situation, to the "normal everyday frame of life," that is, to that grouping of practices that make up the natural history of our species. Having recourse to *regularity*, that is, to the natural-historical "bedrock," fuels two distinct types of innovative action. On the one hand, the regularity legitimizes eccentric, surprising, and inventive applications of the given rule. On the other hand, the regularity can also cause the transformation, and even the abolition, of the rule in question. These two types of creativity are inextricably intertwined. Only by varying its applications, time and time again, can one come to modify, or to substitute a certain rule. It is good to insist on the fact that the two forms of innovation, so intimately correlated with each other, both depend on the tripartite structure of the action: if "to follow a rule" were reduced to a twofold structure of rule/application, and that "system of reference" that is "the common behavior of mankind" were missing from it, there would be no significant deflection from the habitual ways of behaving. Yet, it is necessary to be careful not to identify *regularity* with a super-rule. Doing that would again revive the regression to the infinite that Schmitt and Wittgenstein have dedicated themselves to defusing. *Regularity* is the base, and the condition, of the possibility for distinguishing between grammatical plane (rule) and empirical plane (application); but, precisely for this reason, it is not subjected to these planes. We are dealing, let us repeat, with an area in which indiscernibility rules: the riverbed coincides, here, with the rushing of the water. In order to avoid a misunderstanding about a super-rule, I prefer go in the opposite direction and to balance out the "normal everyday frame of life" with a *pure application*, antecedent to any positive norm.

Jokes reside in a no-man's land that separates a norm from its realization in a particular case. The point of honor of the witty remark lies in its ability to show how many different ways one can apply the same rule. Or, if you prefer: in its ability to show that no application agrees with the rule; nor, after all, does it contradict the rule, given that between one and the other there exists an overwhelming gulf. We can now add that jokes achieve all this because they recap in themselves all the salient traits of the state of exception. Jokes perform a surprise retreat from the *norm* to *normality*, they strip the rule of authority in the name of "the common behavior of mankind," they fuel, without reserve, the indiscernibility between grammatical clauses and empirical clauses. Let us take an example from Freud. A beggar asks a rich baron to help him go to Ostend; his doctors have recommended that he bathe in sea water in order to regain his health. "' Very well,' said the rich man, 'I'll give you something towards it. But must you go precisely to Ostend, which is the most expensive of all sea-bathing resorts?'—"Herr Baron,' was the reproachful reply, 'I consider nothing too expensive for my health'" (Freud: 63–64). In order to justify his impertinent application of the rule that governs the request for a loan, the beggar calls upon that elementary force that is the instinct of self-preservation. It is the "normal everyday frame of life" that suggests unexpected combinations of words and thoughts, irregular inferences, contradictions capable of bewildering and illuminating—"applauded" at the end of his speech, the orator turns towards his friends and asks, "What have I said that's stupid, then?" (ibid: 67). This is the unification of that which seemed unrelated, and the separation of elements considered to be almost symbiotic. Let us consider another example. A horse trader recommends a racehorse to his client: "If you take this horse and get on it at four in the morning you'll be at Pressburg by half-past six."—"What should I be doing in Pressburg at half-past six in the morning?" (ibid: 62). By interrupting a dialog headed elsewhere, like a dramatic turn of events, the witty remark is a *decision*: it truncates, cuts away. If considered in the light of the rule that it also applies, the joke, to say it in Schmitt's language, comes "from the perspective of the content of the underlying norm, new and alien" (Schmitt, *Theology*: 31), the decision-joke "emanates from nothingness" (ibid: 32). Let us clarify, yet again, however, that nothingness-in-the-normative-sense is only the disparaging pseudonym of that *regularity* of vital species-specific behaviors upon which rest the different norms.

The joke is an innovative action that decrees the state of exception. On a par with all other innovative actions, the joke also rises up from the rule to "the common behavior of humankind." Nevertheless, in the case of the joke it is necessary to understand this last notion in a more articulated fashion. We have said that "the common behavior of humankind" is equivalent, roughly, to those fundamental practices that Wittgenstein calls the "natural history" of our species: commanding, interrogating, recounting, elaborating hypotheses, etc. This is true, but it is not the whole story. The regularity preceding the rules consists, in the first place, of the relationship between nonlinguistic drives and verbal behaviors. The regularity does not derive from these drives, but neither can it be reduced to the repeated use of certain words: instead, it becomes one with the *conversion* of the drives into words. What counts is this stitching together as such; this is the precise point in which the language grafts itself on to instinctual reactions and reorganizes them (See Lo Piparo: 19–28). What is common to every life, above all, is the *passage* from the cry of pain to the phrases in which one expresses one's own suffering; the *passage* from silent sexual desire to its articulation in clausal form; the *passage* from perceptive-motor imagination to the metaphors and to the metonymies that mould it from top to bottom. The "normal everyday frame of life" is, above all, this *threshold*: not simply that which follows it. And it is to this threshold that jokes retrace their steps.

The second meaning of "the common behavior of mankind" is inferable from Section 244 of the *Philosophical Investigations*: "Words are connected with the primitive, the natural, expressions of the sensation and used in their place. A child has hurt himself and he cries; and then adults talk to him and teach him exclamations and, later, sentences. They teach the child new pain-behavior. "So you are saying that the word 'pain' really means crying?"—On the contrary: the verbal expression of pain replaces crying and does not describe it" (Wittgenstein, *Investigations*: 75–76). Whatever holds true for pain, holds true also for fear, desire, sympathy and antipathy, submissiveness and dominance. In all these cases, and in others still, the verbal expression does *not* describe the instinctual reaction; *rather*, it substitutes it. Nonetheless, in the moment in which the substitution takes place, an intermediate state prevails: no longer a simple reaction, and not yet a true and actual linguistic game (See De Carolis: 145–50). When the conversion of the verbal cry takes place, the word itself retains something of the instinctive reaction (nonverbal use of verbal language) and the cry is forcefully dragged into the clausal structure (verbal use of nonverbal language). It is naïve to believe that this chasm is confined to an immemorial past. On the contrary: innumerable are the ways in which language calls forth and reiterates within itself (thanks, that is, to sophisticated semantic procedures) the substitution of the instinctive signal on behalf of the verbal expression. Among these various ways, jokes stand out significantly. Whoever coins them undertakes an immediate journey backwards: from the linguistic game currently in progress to the instinctive reaction that it has replaced. Let it be clear: the joke's author does not return to the bare prelinguistic reaction (which by now is already beyond hope); rather, the author returns to the point in which such a reaction is converted into words. This conversion is the core of *regularity*, the deepest layer of "the common behavior of humankind." Freud presents us with a joke whose content illustrates marvelously the implicit structure of numerous jokes: a regression to the threshold at which sensation is usurped by a phrase. This metajoke, which expresses wittily that which other jokes do, is the mirror image of Section 244 of *Philosophical Investigations*. Let us read this metajoke: "The doctor, who had been asked to look after the Baroness at her confinement, pronounced that the moment had not come, and suggested to the Baron that in the meantime they should have a game of cards in the next room. After a while a cry of pain from the Baroness struck the ears of the two men: 'Ah, mon Dieu, que je souffre!' Her husband sprang up, but the doctor signed to him to sit down: 'It's nothing. Let's go on with the game!' A little later there were again sounds from the pregnant woman: 'Mein Gott, mein Gott, what terrible pains!'—'Aren't you going in, Professor?' asked the Baron—'No, no. It's not time yet.'—At last there came from next door an unmistakable cry of 'Aa-ee, aa-ee, aa-ee!' The doctor threw down his cards and exclaimed: 'Now it's time'" (Freud: 95).

The joke is the state of exception of discourse because it suddenly edits, once again, the *primary scene* of every speaker: the grafting of the clausal thought onto nonlinguistic drives. This grafting, I repeat, is not simply an ontogenetic episode, but also a permanent dimension of linguistic experience: that dimension, to put it plainly, in which our words imitate that which they substitute (the cry or whatever), thus resembling a thoughtless reaction. Jokes are habitual dwellers of that dimension. Precisely for this reason, they have the appearance of a *semi-instinctual drive*, or, as Freud says, of an "involuntary idea." Those who coin jokes often do not even imagine what they will say before saying it. But this absence of premeditation attests only to the return to a *regularity* in which the word is joined—still or once again—"with the original, natural expression of the sensation" of desire, of emotion. According to Freud, "The regression of the train of thought to perception is absent in jokes" (ibid.: 205), yet within jokes one can still find "the other two stages of dream-formation, the sinking of a preconscious thought into the unconscious and its unconscious revision" (ibid.: 205). I cannot share this affirmation. It seems to me that jokes return, if not to perception as such, certainly towards the junction between perception and discourse. What we have here, to be sure, is a "sinking," but a "sinking" of verbal thought into the telluric region in which jokes are continuously grafted upon nonlinguistic drives.

The joke is the black box of innovative action: it reproduces in miniature the structure and movements of the action. The transformation of a form of life takes its origin from the uncertainty experienced in applying a rule. This uncertainty urges us to rise up again, at least for a moment (and that moment is the state of exception), to the threshold in which the drives are correlated with linguistic games. The return to the drives implies the possibility of elaborating them in a different manner. The cry of sorrow, or of joy, or of fear, can be *substituted* in unforeseen and inventive ways, in such a way as to modify completely, or in part, the preceding linguistic game (whose rules could barely be applied). An innovative substitution of the instinctive reaction is seen, above all, but not only, in jokes that hinge upon the distortion or overturning of stereotypes and conventional formulas: "We, by the *un*grace of God, day-laborers ..." (ibid., 90). It is seen also in jokes that break words down into their sublexical components: "*Vous m'avez fait connaître un jeune homme 'roux' et 'sot', mais non pas un Rousseau*" [italics mine] (ibid: 31). Useless as their particular contents may seem, these jokes vary the articulation between drives and verbal language in experimental ways. The retreat to *regularity* anticipates also an inverse movement: from regularity to eventual, new rules. The metamorphosis of a cry into words is inevitable but not unambiguous: it is always possible to alter the grammar of sorrow or of desire.

Section 3

Reasoning in a Critical Situation

5

The Logic of Jokes

In the first part of this study (Chapters One and Two) I have tried to define the *nature* of the joke, its identification card. Result: the joke is an innovative action carried out in the public sphere in the presence of neutral spectators. Joke-making inscribes itself entirely within the framework of *práxis*. It entails the use of *phrónesis*, that is to say, of practical know-how that allows us to assess what it is appropriate to carry out within a possible situation. *Práxis* and *phrónesis*, however, pushed to the extreme, since the joke is an action that undermines and contradicts the prevalent belief-system of a community (*éndoxa*), thus revealing the transformability of the contemporary form of life. In the second part of this study (Chapters Three and Four), I attempted to retrace the *structure* of jokes and of innovative action in general, the internal dynamics that distinguish the ways in which they function. Result: a joke applies a rule to a particular instance and in this way it highlights the persistent disconnect (rather, the incommensurability) between a rule and its application. The structure of a joke mimics the typical movement of *decision-making*: in order to establish, in each instance, how to enforce a norm, it is necessary to move beyond this norm, to connect to "the common behavior of mankind." Now, in the concluding part of my study, it is fitting to examine closely the *logic* of jokes and of innovative action, the tools used in jokes for breaking through acquired habits and for introducing a diversion in behavior. At stake here are the argumentative models at work in joke-telling, the inferences through which this joke-telling applies a rule in a surprising manner and decrees the state of exception of linguistic praxis.

Freud classifies jokes according to the peculiar phonetic, semantic and logical resources from which they take their origin. First of all, he identifies two large groupings, almost visible to the naked eye: on one side, "linguistic jokes"; on the other, "conceptual jokes." We should not assume that the conceptual jokes are, even in small measure, independent from the act of speaking. Joke-telling is always a purely linguistic action. The difference between verbal and conceptual is, rather, the difference between signifier and signified. Verbal jokes play on the material body of one simple expression, or of an entire enunciation; conceptual jokes play on the interrelatedness of semantic contents (See Todorov: 248–250). With regard to the verbal joke, it seems that all is played out "in focusing our psychical attitude upon the *sound* of the word instead of upon its *meaning*—in making the (acoustic) word-presentation itself take the place of its significance as given by its relations to thing-presentation" (Freud, *Jokes*: 146). With regard to the conceptual, the dominating impression is that of witnessing the abrupt coming together of unrelated, even incoherent thoughts; this coming together would not be lacking much of anything important if it were to be articulated with a different turn of phrase.

Freud himself repeatedly comments on how fragile and reversible this division can be: we run into it in every step of the way, in jokes that belong to both sides of the imaginary divide. It is virtually impossible, for instance, to decide if a double entendre is "verbal" or "conceptual," if it hinges upon the signifier or the signified; just as it is not our prerogative to separate, at first, the witty act of begging the question from the repeated utilization of its articulated sound ("*Experience* consists in experiencing what we do not wish to *experience*" (ibid: 77 [italics mine]). Certainly, there are some jokes that fall apart as soon as their expressive form is modified (the "famillionairy" benevolence of Rothshield); and there are jokes that outlast being paraphrased (the penniless man who uses all the money loaned to him to stuff himself on salmon). These are more or less accentuated fluctuations around a center of gravity over which presides the indissoluble nexus between the choice of the "right word" and the development of an irregular inference. Keeping our eyes fixed upon this center of gravity, let us explore the *logical form* that relates the two large groupings of jokes, as well as their species and subspecies (condensation, double entendre, displacement, unification, indirect figuration, etc.), since Freud has dedicated nearly a third of his book to these taxonomies. Only the identification of this logical form will allow for a different foundation to the classification of witty retorts.

All jokes, including the simple play on words based on alliteration, are modes of *reasoning*, with premises and conclusions (regardless of whether they are explicit or implicit). They are, however, formally *erroneous* modes of reasoning, whose outcome depends upon unfounded presuppositions, semantic ambiguities, defective correlations, arbitrary amplification or arbitrary limitation of elements to be considered, shameless transgression of the principle of the "excluded middle" (*principium tertii exclusi* or *tertium non datur*). The logical form of jokes seems to be, therefore, an argumentative fallacy. Jokes resemble apparent syllogisms or incorrect syllogisms. Apparent syllogisms, if they originate from false premises, that is to say, from simply hypothetical *éndoxa*, drawing conclusions opposite to those of actually viable *éndoxa*. Incorrect syllogisms, if they originate from true premises, that is to say, from the most dependable *éndoxa*, deriving insidious or surreptitious consequences that, in any case, clash with their point of departure. In either case, jokes are grounded on an eccentric inference. At least at first sight, a joke is an authentic *paralogism*. Later on we shall ascertain that this matter is a lot more complicated. For the time being, it is fitting to assume the kinship between jokes and argumentative fallacy. And to investigate it in all of its details.

Aristotle analyzes the erroneous thought processes that provide the skeleton of a witty retort (and of innovative action) in his treatise *On Sophistical Refutations*. This work is the keystone to our understanding of the logical form of jokes. Of all jokes, let us be clear: not only the form of the endangered subcategory that Freud labeled with the symptomatic epithet of "a piece of sophistry" (ibid: 71). Aristotle subdivides forms of paralogistic reasoning into two principal classes: those that are "connected with language" (*pará ten léxin*) and those that remain "unconnected with language" (*éxo tes léxeos*) (Aristotle, *Refutations*: 19). As we can see, this is the same bipartition used by Freud in relation to jokes: verbal paralogisms and conceptual paralogisms. With one essential difference: in the Aristotelian text, even the play on words, which hinges on the relation among signifiers, is considered a veritable form of *argumentation* capable of altering the direction of thoughts (while Freud reserves this role exclusively for "conceptual" jokes). The pairing of logical fallacies to jokes is not a mere hypothesis; it is corroborated, in the long run, by some objective consonance. In the next to the last chapter of his treatise, Aristotle spells out the connection between mistaken inferences, in particular those that hinge upon homonymy and "humorous phrases" (*oi lógoi ghéloioi*). He relates, in sequence, five jokes that could also figure as tassels of a sophistic argument. For instance: "the man got the cart down from the stand" [*díphros* means both "cart" and "stool"] (ibid: 19; see also Aristotle, *Rhetoric*: 238–239). Here we are in the presence of witty paralogism, paralogistic wit: in some cases, we should speak of complete juxtaposition rather than of relationships.

It would be meaningless, at this point, to go back over the details of the various argumentative fallacies. What matters is giving a broad identity to the formal machinery that characterizes each of them. In this way, we can also confidently identify this machinery in a successful joke or in the unusual way in which a rule is applied to a particular case. The *organon* of innovative action is constituted by a certain number of irregular or "incorrect" inferences. In order to acquire a minimal familiarity with this *organon*, it is sufficient to have a well thought-out list of the principal verbal and conceptual fallacies that take root in those inferences. I will proceed in this manner: I will place alongside a brief definition of a paralogism (derived from Aristotle) one or two jokes (mentioned by Freud) that exemplify, in their own way, the peculiar mechanism of the paralogism.

Fallacies Based upon Language (*pará ten léxin*):

1. *Equivocation.* The ambiguity of a single term leads to a paradoxical conclusion. Aristotelian example: since the expression "must exist" means "what is necessary" as well as "morally proper," the sophist asserts that "evils are good, for what must exist is good, and evil must exist" (Aristotle, *Refutations*: 19). *Corresponding jokes: a)* "This girl reminds me of Dreyfus. The army doesn't believe in her innocence" (Freud, *Jokes*: 44); *b) "C'est le premier vol*

['flight' but also 'theft'] *de l'aigle*," which was said about Napoleon's thievery and rapaciousness when he first seized power (ibid: 40 [italics mine]).

2. *Ambiguity*. The ambiguity concerns an entire sentence, since the word order does not distinguish between subject and object. Aristotelian example: "to wish me the enemy to capture" (it remains uncertain whether one wishes to be captured by the enemies or to capture them) (Aristotle, *Refutations*: 19). *Corresponding jokes: a)* "Two Jews met ... 'Have you taken a bath?' asked one of them. 'What?' asked the other in return, 'is there one missing?'" (Freud, *Jokes*: 55); *b)* "A doctor, as he came away from a lady's bedside, said to her husband with a shake of his head: 'I don't like her looks.' 'I've not liked her looks for a long time', the husband hastened to agree" (ibid: 41).

3. *Combination*. This fallacy consists of assuming "in combination," as an indivisible monolith, that which the speaker has stated in a "divided sense," that is to say, implying an articulation or a progression. Aristotelian example: when someone says that "A man can walk while sitting," the sophist who does not separate the before from the after, or potentiality from actuality, infers that the man in question can walk *while* he is sitting (Aristotle, *Refutations*: 21). *Corresponding joke*: "A gentleman entered a pastry-cook's shop and ordered a cake; but he soon brought it back and asked for a glass of liqueur instead. He drank it and began to leave without having paid. The proprietor detained him. 'What do you want?' asked the customer.—'You've not paid for the liqueur.'—'But I gave you the cake in exchange for it.'—'You didn't pay for that either.'—'But I hadn't eaten it'" (Freud, *Jokes*: 66).

4. *Division*. Symmetrical with the previous fallacy, this one consists in understanding, in a divided sense, that which the speaker

has stated in compound terms. Aristotelian example: whoever answers affirmatively the sophist's inquiry as to whether "5 is 2 and 3" will receive the following retort from the sophist: "5 is odd and even" (Aristotle, *Refutations*: 23). *Corresponding joke*: "The *Shadchen* [the broker] was defending the girl he had proposed against the young man's protests. 'I don't care for the mother in law', said the latter. 'She's a disagreeable, stupid person.'—'But after all you're not marrying the mother-in-law. What you do want is the daughter.'—'Yes, but she's not young any longer, and she's not precisely a beauty.'—'No matter. If she is neither young nor beautiful she'll be all the more faithful to you.'—'And she hasn't much money.'—'Who's talking about money? Are you marrying money then? After all it's a wife that you want.'—'But she's got a hunchback too.' 'Well, what *do* you want? Isn't she to have a single fault?'" (Freud, *Jokes*: 71).

5. *Form of expression.* In this instance, what we have is a surreptitious exchange between clearly distinct categories, an exchange that produces an erroneous inference (quantity in place of quality, space in place of time, etc.). Undeniably, this is due to the ambiguous manner in which we express ourselves. Aristotelian example (in which the category of quantity is replaced by the category of substance): the sophist asks if it is correct to maintain that he who had something and now does not have it must have lost that which he once had. Having obtained an affirmative answer, the sophist points out that if someone used to possess ten dice and loses one, he no longer possesses the ten dice that he could have used before and concludes that, as a result, this man has lost all ten dice. (Aristotle, *Refutations*: 111). *Corresponding joke* (centered on the paralogical exchange between the category of reality and the category of possibility): "The would-be bridegroom complained that the

bride had one leg shorter than the other and limped. The *Schadchen* contradicted him: 'You are wrong. Suppose you marry a woman with healthy, straight limbs! What do you gain from it? You never have a day's security that she won't fall down, break a leg and afterward be lame all her life. And think of the suffering then, the agitation, and the doctor's bill! But if you take *this* one, that can't happen to you. Here you have a *fait accompli*" (Freud, *Jokes*: 72).

Fallacies Independent of Language (*éxo ten léxin*):

1. *Fallacies connected with accident.* The mistake lies in attributing to the grammatical subject all that can be attributed to its accidental predicates. Aristotelian example: Socrates is white; white is a color that blurs vision; thus Socrates is a color that blurs vision (Aristotle, *Refutations*: 27). *Corresponding jokes*: "This lady resembles the Venus of Milo in many respects: she, too, is extraordinarily old, like her she has no teeth, and there are white patches on the yellowish surface of her body" (Freud, *Jokes*: 82); *b)* "He united in himself the characteristics of the greatest men. He carried his head askew like Alexander; he always had to wear a *toupet* like Caesar; he could drink coffee like Leibnitz; and once he was properly settled in his armchair, he forgot eating and drinking like Newton, and had to be woken up like him; he wore his wig like Dr. Johnson, and he always left a breeches-button undone like Cervantes" (ibid: 82).

2. *Fallacies in which an expression is considered absolute, when it is instead qualified as to manner or place or time or relation.* This fallacy (closest to the "combinational" fallacy reviewed above) exists when we arbitrarily lead the metaphorical back to its literal meaning. Aristotelian examples: *a)* If what does not exist is the object of an opinion, then that which does not exist, is (Aristotle, *Refutations*: 27); *b)* An Ethiopian, being completely black, is white in respect to his teeth; then the Ethiopian is both white and not white (ibid: 27).

Corresponding jokes: "A horse-dealer was recommending a saddle-horse to a customer. If you take this horse and get on it at four in the morning you'll be at Pressburg by half-past six.'—'What should I be doing in Pressburg at half-past six in the morning?'" (Freud, *Jokes*: 62); "'How are you getting along?' the blind man asked the lame man. 'As you see', the lame man replied to the blind man" (ibid: 37); "It is almost impossible the carry the torch of truth through a crowd without singeing someone's beard" (ibid: 97).

3. *Fallacies connected with ignorance of the nature of refutation.* If predicate B is undetermined, or if we first point out its definitive aspect and then an accidental one, we can maintain both that "A is B" and that "A is not B," thus violating the principle of *tertium non datur*. Aristotelian example: the sophist maintains that "two is double and not double" for two is double of one, but not double of three (Aristotle, *Refutations*: 29). *Corresponding joke*: "The *Schadchen* had assured the suitor that the girl's father was no longer living. After the betrothal it emerged that the father was still alive and was serving a prison sentence. The suitor protested to the *Schadchen*, who replied: 'Well, what did I tell you? You surely don't call that living?'" (Freud, *Jokes*: 62–63).

4. *Fallacies connected with the assumption of the original point to be proved.* This very famous fallacy consists in assuming what needs to be demonstrated as the premise of one's inference. Aristotelian example: medicine can tell a functioning organ apart from an ailing one, thus medicine is the science of heath and disease (Aristotle, *Topica*: 731). *Corresponding joke*: "Experience consists in experiencing what we do not wish to experience" (Freud, *Jokes*: 77).

5. *Fallacy connected with the consequent.* It is not correct to assume symmetry between condition and conditioned: the latter

derives from the first, but not vice versa. Aristotelian example: "men often take" something for honey "because a yellow colour accompanies honey" (Aristotle, *Refutations*: 31): this statement cannot be converted to "if it is yellow it is honey." *Corresponding joke*: "A man who had taken to drink supported himself by tutoring in a small town. His vice gradually became known, however, and as a result he lost most of his pupils. A friend was commissioned to urge him to mend his ways. 'Look, you could get the best tutoring in town if you would give up drinking. So do give up!' 'Who do you think you are?' was the indignant reply. 'I do tutoring so that I can drink. Am I to give up drinking so that I can get tutoring?'" (Freud, *Jokes*: 59).

6

Alternative Combinations and Deviated

Trajectories: The Resources of Innovative Action

The argumentative fallacies analyzed by Aristotle are the logical form of jokes and of innovative action. Everything depends on understanding whether we can still speak of "fallacies" when we are dealing with a joke or an innovative action. I do not believe so. I believe that the paralogism, while safeguarding in its entirety its formal prerogatives, ceases to be a logical error once the conditions of its use (and consequently its previous functions) have changed. The goal of the next chapter will be to unravel this issue. Meanwhile, I would not like for a potentially dangerous misconception to take over: it is not my intention to propose that, in order to do something new, we need to rely on disconnected and flawed reasoning. In order to avert such discreditable misgiving, I must introduce, even before returning to the major thread of my argument, two considerations that will begin to clarify how and why, in certain circumstances, an "erroneous" inference is anything but an error.

The paralogisms examined in Aristotle's *On Sophistical Refutations* pertain to descriptive statements. They lead to deceptive conclusions on one or another state of things in the world. So then, here is our first consideration: those same paralogisms, when they figure as the *organon* of jokes and of innovative action, become, instead, the main ingredient of *counterfactual reasoning*. That is, they contribute to elaborating a hypothesis about what would happen if conditions other than those at hand were to prevail, if certain empirical data were to vary, if other *éndoxa* or other rules were in place. The forms of reasoning in question avail themselves of a protasis in the subjunctive ("if only Oswald had not killed Kennedy"), that runs *counter to factual evidence,* and they avail themselves as well of an apodosis in the conditional ("then the United States would not have become trapped in the Vietnam war") that serves to spell out the inferable consequences to that conscious alteration of known reality. When linguistic praxis is forced to become familiar with a state of exception, paralogisms allow for the verbalization of blatantly false proteses in the subjunctive, upon which the conditional individuation of innovative actions depend. For instance, *if* we were to understand in a combined way that which is uttered in a divided manner, *then* I would behave this way or that; *if* the grammatical subject were intrinsically linked to all that pertains to its accidental predicates, *then* there would emerge an aspect of the issue which has been thus far ignored or there would be an opening for a cutting joke. The counterfactual premise (almost always *counternormative,* to be specific) can turn out to be perspicuous or trivial, fertile or gratuitous, but under no circumstance can it be "fallacious."

The second consideration is just an amplification of the previous one. Connecting that which is divided, or dividing that which is connected, is certainly illegitimate if we want to corroborate a given hypothesis, but it absolutely is not illegitimate if we are striving to formulate a new hypothesis. In as much as they lay down the foundations of jokes and of transformative praxis, "fallacies" reveal some affinities with the methodology employed by mathematicians to formulate new theorems. The *logic of discovery* diverges from the *logic of justification* because it must do away with deductive demonstration and it relies, at times, upon completely irresponsible tools, such as analogy and the hybridization of heterogeneous contexts. In a wonderful new book, published recently, Carlo Cellucci has thoroughly discussed the various types of inference employed in the research of innovative hypotheses in mathematics. Some of these inferences are the heuristic counter-figures (that is, within the logic of discovery) of those argumentative methods that, when applied to the logic of justification, should doubtlessly be labeled as fallacies or paralogisms. Let us give two examples. First, the *metaphor*: for the mathematician it "is the claim that objects of a given domain, called the primary domain, are objects of another domain, called the secondary domain. Since the objects of the secondary domain have a certain property, we conclude, by way of metaphor, that also the objects of the primary domain have the same property" (Cellucci: 270). The transferring of property from one domain to the other veils a truly innovative hypothesis only when it concerns the most idiosyncratic properties, that is to say, the most specific and apparently the least sharable properties of the secondary domain. In Aristotelian terms: the innovative hypothesis emerges when we ascribe to the grammatical subject also the *accidental* properties of its predicate (fallacy "of accident"). The other example is that of the *variation of data*: this methodology consists in modifying, wholly or in part, the initial terms of a problem, so as to move gradually forward from one problem to an entirely different problem (Cellucci: 292–295). This is what happens (but in the form of a malicious error, because, within that context, the logic of justification is at stake) in many of the sophistic paralogisms examined by Aristotle: here we should think about equivocation and ambiguity, but also about fallacies connected to ignorance of the nature of refutation.

While one single argumentative procedure is paralogistic within a descriptive statement, it is still, however, legitimate, and at times even useful, within the context of counterfactual reasoning. While one single inference is fallacious within the logic of justification, it becomes productive and even indispensable within the logic of discovery. It is unnecessary to add that, in place of "counterfactual reasoning" and of the "logic of discovery," we could easily interchange "joke" and "unconventional application of a rule." These indications serve as a warning and a safety measure against potential misunderstandings. However, I repeat, only later (see Chapter Seven) will I clarify the fundamental condition where a paralogism ceases to be *necessarily* an error (and to be paralogistic, because, subject to a vicious circle, it is the opinion of those who keep considering it erroneous). For the time being, it is enough to put mental quotation marks around the terms fallacies and erroneous reasoning as we proceed to discuss them.

Only at this point does it become possible to unravel the crucial question, that has been set aside for too long now: how can we subdivide the varieties of jokes, given that the partitioning of jokes into "verbal" and "conceptual" realms is tenuous, even deceptive, and is contradicted by countless amphibian fallacies? The classification of jokes (and also, by holding them up to the light, of innovative actions) inevitably starts with their logical form. As we have seen, all jokes, even those in which the material body of the word plays a crucial role, are forms of *argumentation*. Or, better yet: irregular argumentation, akin to apparent or incorrect syllogism, is always based on anomalous inferences. Such a subdivision must assess the argumentative strategy inherent to jokes (and to transformative praxis). If the logical form of jokes is a sophistic fallacy, it is within this fallacy that we must search for unique characteristics and articulations.

The forms of paralogistic reasoning analyzed by Aristotle in his *Sophistical Refutations* can be divided into two principal groupings. These groupings have nothing to do with the paired signifier/signified, but are, rather, characterized by different inferential techniques.

a) On one side, we can group together paralogisms (and the jokes that derive from them) whose common distinctive trait lies in *the different combination of the elements given in their origin.* The different combination makes it possible for two contrasting meanings to openly coexist in one enunciation: argumentation fluctuates from one to another meaning and in the end it is the least obvious and the most polemical that prevails. This class of paralogism draws on the permanent rift that was analyzed by Émile Benveniste, between *semiotic* field (system of signs) and *semantic* field (universe of discourse): there are, in fact, two divergent semantic, yet simultaneous, realizations that originate in the same semiotic material. Every statement of facts and of the state of things is simultaneously a statement on the use of words: what we witness, thus, is a complete fusion of language-object and of metalanguage. The following paralogisms belong, probably, to this first grouping: homonimy, amphiboly, composition, division, within those paralogisms "based on expression"; begging the question and fallacy of false cause, within those that are "independent from expression."

b) On the other hand, we have fallacies (and their corresponding jokes) that share the tendency to *deviate from the axis of discourse so as to introduce heterogeneous elements that were not previously considered.* We discuss this issue in such a way as to move away from the constellation of thoughts that lead dialogue up to that point, and also to shift our attention quickly to a collateral theme. We find ourselves in the presence of plethoric syllogisms, since these syllogisms avail themselves of a more or less hidden *third premise*, one that is capable of directing the conclusion toward problems or possibilities up to now ignored. We change the subject without showing it. And we change it through a peculiar violation of the principle of the "excluded middle": faced with the alternatives "A is white" or "A is not white," we suppose that it is totally clear to remark that "A is ... tall." The paratactic "is," privileged over the disjunctive "or," allows us to multiply the number of variables that need to be kept mind in the course of our argument. This second grouping includes the *pará ten léxin* paralogism, that arises from the inappropriate superimposition of different categories (substance/quantity, reality/possibility, etc.) and the remaining *éxo tes léxeos* paralogisms: fallacies connected by accident, fallacies in which an expression is used absolutely, or not absolutely, but qualified as to manner or place or time or relation, fallacies connected with ignorance of the nature of refutation.

According to the Freudian taxonomy of jokes, the diverse combination of given elements bears the description of *multiple use of the same material*, while the deviation from the axis of discourse is designated as *displacement of psychic emphasis*. We should not be deceived by the apparent assonance. For Freud, in fact, these are only particular subspecies: multiple usages represent a circumscribed case of "conceptual joke." What is now capsized is the relation between part and whole. The coupling of multiple use/displacement supersedes, as a general principle of classification, the coupling of verbal/conceptual. Each one of the two new polarities thus includes both jokes in which the signifier is of primary importance, and jokes that hinge entirely on their semantic content (provided we want to preserve at all cost this dubious distinction). This different criterion of categorization of jokes explicitly underlines the nexus that unites these jokes as forms of argumentative fallacy. The absolute supremacy achieved by the coupling multiple/displacement is a repercussion of Aristotle's *On Sophistical Refutations* within the Freudian context of *Witz*. To allow this repercussion to take place, however, is a theoretical choice.

The subdivision of jokes (and, prior to this, of irregular reasoning) into the two main groupings of "multiple use of the same material" and "displacement of psychic accent" attempts to address without much hesitation the original question—that has been consistently brought back to the fore: what are the *logicolinguistic resources* of innovative action? I maintain that all jokes, as well as all endeavors to modify one's form of life in a critical situation, are nourished *either* by the unusual combination of given elements *or* by an abrupt deviation towards ulterior elements, which are more or less incoherent with respect to the initial order of discourse. Both of these resources, which must be understood as distinct articulations of the same logical form, assert themselves fully in the state of exception of linguistic praxis. The multiple use of the same material and the displacement of psychic accent are the two fundamental ways of reacting to the intensifying of chronic problems presented by the application of a rule to a particular case. Furthermore: these are the two ways in which, in the process of their application, we return to the primary system of reference that is the "common behavior of mankind." Multiple use and displacement are the two main genres of fallacy and the primary genres of jokes. However, as we have just seen, in jokes (as well as in the unusual application of a rule) fallacies have the value of counterfactual hypotheses, and therefore they take shape as heuristic procedures. To sum up, we are dealing with *productive* fallacies, whose function is to vary a linguistic game or a lifestyle. The subdivision I have just proposed refers specifically to *this* use of paralogistic inferences.

The two types of jokes (as well as productive fallacy) correspond to two types of creative action on a vast scale. The multiple use of the same material has its macroscopic equivalent in *entrepreneurial innovation* (within a meaning of the term "entrepreneur" that is quite distinct from the sickening and odious meaning of the word that is prevalent among the apologists of the capitalistic mode of production).

Displacement constitutes, instead, the logicolinguistic resource of a political experience that has marked, with varying results, our entire tradition: *exodus.* Let us closely consider this double nexus between verbal microcosm and historicosocial macrocosm.

(A) *Entrepreneurial innovation*

Joseph Schumpeter, one of the few 20th century authors who has been bold enough to analyze industrial economy as "total social fact" (within the wide-ranging point of view of an anthropologist), has elaborated a significant theory of innovation at the heart of which stands an "entrepreneurial function" seen as a basically human aptitude.

According to Schumpeter, it would be a mistake to confuse the entrepreneur with the CEO of a capitalistic enterprise, or even worse, with its owner. What we have here is not a socially defined role; rather, it is a species-specific faculty that becomes activated in the case of crisis or stagnation. Stated differently, the entrepreneur

is every linguistic animal: but every linguistic animal is only spo-
radically, intermittently entrepreneurial: "being an entrepreneur is
not a profession and as a rule not a lasting condition" (Schumpeter:
78). Schumpeter also outlines a clear separation in relation to the
figure of the inventor: while the latter adds some novel element to
the productive process, the entrepreneur stakes all her/his chips on
the *polysemy* of the already available elements. S/he breaks with the
"state of equilibrium" and differently combines elements that have
been available all along, since the beginning, without having any
singular significance. At stake here is not the quantity or the quality
of productive factors, but the modification of their form. Schumpeter writes: "development consists primarily in employing existing
resources in a different way, in doing new things with them, irre-
spective of whether those resources increase or not" (ibid: 68). The
multiple use of the same material, aside from realizing previously
unforeseen objectives, forges a new way of taking action: "the
conduct in question ... is directed towards something different and
signifies doing something different from *other conduct*" (ibid: 81
[italics mine]).

The entrepreneurial function described by Schumpeter entails
the counterfactual use of an amphiboly ("to wish me the enemy to
capture"; what would happen if the accent were to fall upon the
temptation to surrender instead of falling upon the longing for
victory?), or of a conversion between consequent and antecedent
(what new combination would be obtained by switching from "if
x, then y" to "if y, then x"?). This function is exposed in com-
pendium by the jokes based on *ars combinatoria*, that is, on the
varied utilization of the same verbal material. It is legitimate to
attribute the typical qualities of the entrepreneur described by
Schumpeter to the person capable of coining such jokes: "Some

people think that the husband has earned a lot and so has been able to lay by a bit; others again think that the wife has lain back a bit and so has been able to earn a lot." (Freud, *Jokes*: 35); "Vous m'avez fait connaître un jeune homme *roux* et *sot*, mais non pas un *Rousseau*" [You have made me acquainted with a young man who is red haired and silly, but not a Rousseau] (ibid: 31).

(B) *Exodus*

Exodus is a collective action that hinges on the paralogistic principle of the *tertium datur*. Instead of submitting to the pharaoh or openly rebelling against his rule (A or not A), the Israelites identify another possibility, one which evades the number of alternatives that could be counted at the beginning: that of fleeing Egypt. Neither A, nor not-A, neither resigned acquiescence nor struggle to seize power in a predetermined territory, but an eccentric B, achievable only as long as other premises are surreptitiously introduced into the given syllogism. The separation from the "house of slavery and of unjust toil" takes place in the precise moment in which *a side road*, unchartered on sociopolitical maps, is identified.

Exodus is not different from *changing topic* while a conversation is already directed on well-defined tracks. Instead of choosing what it is best to do starting from certain basic conditions, we endeavor to modify these conditions, that is, to modify the very "grammar" that determines the selection of all possible choices. Exodus is the transfer to political praxis of the heuristic procedure, which we have mentioned above and which the mathematicians define as "variation of data": giving precedence to secondary or heterogeneous factors, we move gradually from a determined problem: subjection or insurrection, to a totally different problem:

how to realize a defection and to experience forms of self-government that were previously inconceivable.

In the past I have systematically discussed the political model of exodus, its extraordinary pertinence to a time when the crisis of the modern State is unfolding. (See Virno, "Virtuosismo" and *Esercizi*; and also, from a partially different perspective: De Carolis, *Tempo*; and Mezzadra.) In that context, what was important was to provide some account of the logicolinguistic resources requisite for the human animal, in order for this animal to be able to change the very context within which a conflict takes place, rather than remaining within that conflict and acting in accordance with one or the other of the behaviors intrinsic to that conflict. Well then, the logicolinguistic resources required to open up an unforeseen way out of Pharaoh's Egypt are the same resources that nurture jokes (and paralogistic inferences) characterized by *displacement*, that is to say, by an abrupt deviation in the axis of discourse. The skeletal structure of the exodus is faithfully reproduced, though in Lilliputian dimensions, by the countless jokes I have examined before. Let us recall at least one of them. A gentleman in financial distress obtains a small loan from an acquaintance. The following day, his benefactor chances upon him in a restaurant eating salmon and mayonnaise. The gentleman reprimands him resentfully: "'Is that what you've used my money for?' 'I don't understand you', replied the object of the attack; 'if I haven't any money I can't eat salmon mayonnaise, and if I have some money I mustn't eat salmon mayonnaise. Well, then, when am I to eat salmon mayonnaise?'" (Freud: 56).

7

On the Crisis of a Form of Life

Any attempt at reconstructing the logic of innovative action is headed for inevitable failure, if it does not assess the width and depth of the field within which such action takes its roots: *the crisis of a form of life.* Only by means of this assessment, which must be calibrated with the precision of a land-surveyor, can one grasp the condition that allows argumentative fallacies to evolve into sober heuristic instruments.

A theory of crisis must develop to the full that which we have stated with regard to the application of a rule and to the state of exception in which linguistic praxis at times comes to a head (see Chapter Four). A form of life withers and declines when the same norm is realized in multiple dissimilar ways that contrast with one another. Forced to suspend or to discredit the rule in question, we resort to the "common behavior of mankind," that is, to the *regularity* of aptitudes and of species-specific conduct. This regularity, placed ahead of any system of positively determined rules, is human life when it is on the verge (but only on the verge) of assuming one form or another. It is the "layer of rock" that lies, mostly hidden, beneath the varying linguistic games that follow one after the other in the course of time. The crisis of a particular form of life reintroduces the problem of *shaping* life in general, because it brings to the surface, in a particular historical moment and with constantly varying modalities, the metahistorical "layer of rock." The *regularity* to which we return when our previous habits perish is characterized, from a logical point of view, by the most radical inscrutability of environments and levels. In the state of exception, any effort to distinguish the rule from its application is in vain (we can, at the most, state, with a patent paradox, that the rule is only … a particular case of its own application). When the "common behavior of mankind" becomes the main system of reference, there is a blurring of all reliable demarcation between background and foreground, of unquestionable presuppositions and contingent phenomena, of grammatical level and empirical level. This or that fact of life (empirical level) can thicken at any moment into a norm (grammatical level), while the norms previously in force are now liquefying, so as to take on again the guise of simple facts of life. To anticipate immediately the salient point, we could say: it is the blurring between grammatical and empirical planes, provoked by the crisis of a determined form of life, that makes it possible for the paralogisms examined by Aristotle in his study *On Sophistical Refutations* to cease to be paralogistic and, instead, to become the *organon* of innovative action.

Wittgenstein offers us some limited clues about the ways in which a habit and a linguistic game corrode one another until they perish. Of course, he never fails to underscore the plurality, even the diachronic plurality, of the forms of life, their alternation and their discontinuity: "But what men consider reasonable or unreasonable *alters*. At certain periods men find reasonable what at other periods they found unreasonable. And vice-versa." (Wittgenstein, *Certainty*: 43e [italics mine]). Only rarely, though, does he concentrate on the aspect that really counts: what takes place during the transition from one form of life to the next, in the gray zone where the first form of life barely persists and the second still resembles an eccentric experiment. The effect of Wittgenstein's parsimoniousness in this regard is that many Wittgensteinians, seeing the historicity of the human animal as an ethylic invention of Hegel, resign themselves to recording the periodic shift in collective habits and linguistic games, with the nonchalance of one who makes a little bouquet of colorful flowers or who witnesses the changing of the seasons. History, which is a *natural* prerogative of our species, no less than walking upright, will remain neglected by these imaginary naturalists as long as they do not perceive the necessity of investigating the *crisis* of a form of life. The thread of human historicity is entirely enclosed in the movement by means of which we pass from one grammar to another: it ends up being unintelligible, therefore, for those who compile already constituted and not yet particular grammars. The blindness of a great number of Wittgensteinians makes it even more important to ponder the rare passages in which Wittgenstein, rather than limiting himself to acknowledging the variability of the forms of life, outlines a phenomenology and, above all, a *logic* of their crisis. Let us repeat that the task of integrating and clarifying the logic of innovative action belongs precisely to the logic of crisis.

In addition to paragraph 206 of the *Philosophical Investigations* ("But what if one person reacts in one way and another in another to the order and the training? Which one is right?"), the place in which Wittgenstein presents the most important indications on the state of exception of linguistic praxis is found within a group of observations that, edited during the final two years of his life, were later published under the title *On Certainty*. In these passages he examines specifically the gray zone (regularity) where the grammatical fabric of a form of life (rules) becomes fragile to the point of flowing back to the context of empirical phenomena, while some other empirical phenomena (unusual applications) begin, with an inverted movement, to carry out a grammatical role. If we are to find in Wittgenstein a theory of history, it is here that we must look for it. I am going to focus on three issues: *a)* the reason why grammatical clauses, those pertaining to the foundation of a linguistic game, are neither true not false; *b)* the juxtaposition between grammatical level and empirical level (that is, the crisis proper); *c)* the ways in which a new grammar subsumes an older one. All three of these issues contribute to the delineation of the context in which irregular inferences can no longer be taken as "fallacies." As is by now evident, these final pages have the task of recapitulating the main threads of the argument that I have so far explored on jokes as diagram of innovative action. This task will be carried out, I hope, in the only way that escapes the simple compulsion to repeat: by introducing some further nuance that can shed new light on what we have said already.

a) Wittgenstein critically ponders the opinion put forth by George E. Moore. According to this opinion, each individual is in possession of a certain number of propositions that are unfailingly *true*, that are based on something we *know* with absolute certainty. For example: "I know that I have two hands even when I am not paying attention to it," or "the Earth existed before I was born." Wittgenstein's objection is rather harsh: in such cases, he says, the predicate "true" and the verb "to know" are wholly incongruous, even nonsensical. To lay claim to the use of such propositions is a patent logical mistake. The certainty I hold with regard to the existence of my hands has nothing to do with a cognitive act (that is, with a form of knowledge), nor does it derive from a judgment (true or false). Propositions that express a series of unquestionable truths epitomize the *background* against which each act of cognition and each judgment stand out: the presupposition, that is, which makes possible the same distinction between true and false, right and wrong, correct and fallacious. Wittgenstein: "But I did not get my picture of the world by satisfying myself of its correctness; nor do I have it because I am satisfied of its correctness. No: it is the inherited background against which I distinguish between true and false" (ibid: 15e [italics mine]). The certainties that have attracted the attention of Moore cannot be defined true-or-false for a purely logical reason: just like the signs we use to indicate conjunction and negation, they are part of the grammar of a linguistic game; that is, they are comparable to rules: "The propositions describing this world-picture might be part of a kind of *mythology*. And their role is like that of *rules of a game*" (ibid: 15e [italics mine]). A rule cannot be evaluated with the criteria that we utilize for the individual steps of a game, since those criteria (for instance "correctness" or "incorrectness") are derived from that game. "I have a world-picture. Is it true or false? Above all it is the substratum of all my enquiring and asserting" (ibid: 23e).

It would be totally wrong to suppose that grammatical clauses concern only some naturalistic and metahistorical evidence: the parts of the human body, generations following one another, the size and age of the world, and so forth. It is not so. For Wittgenstein, the rules of a linguistic game are none other than "empirical propositions ... hardened" (ibid: 15e). But the possibility of hardening, that is, of ascending to the rank of grammatical units of measure, applies to *every* type of empirical proposition. It applies to "I know that I have two hands," but also to "submission to authority is ingrained in human nature," or to "God created the world." The grammar of a life-form, that is to say "the substratum of all my searching and of all my assertions," consists, in great measure of opinions and historicosocial beliefs. Or, if we prefer, consists of the *éndoxa* ingrained within a determined community. And it is these certainties-*éndoxa* that return to a fluid state in the case of a crisis, thus regaining an empirical tonality. Wittgenstein's example (ibid: 43e, paragraph 336): religious certainty, which was once neither true nor false because it constituted the basis of true and false assertions, has been deemed, from a certain point forward, disputable and even unreasonable.

One does not frequently outline explicitly the grammatical presuppositions of a linguistic game. Normally, no one states: "It is true, I really have two hands." For Wittgenstein, the background acquires maximum significance exclusively in two instances: in ethics and in self-evident jokes. When we wonder about the meaning of life, distancing ourselves for a while from familiar behaviors, it can happen that we "wonder at the existence of the world" (Wittgenstein, "Ethics": 12). It would be nonsensical to say "I *know* that the world exists," since the existence of the world represents the indisputable basis of each effective form of "knowledge." This grammatical certainty, in itself neither true nor false, comes to the fore and provokes a genuine astonishment when I perceive, during an ethical awakening, the divide that separates it from any description of the empirical states of things. A plebeian version of the wonder provoked by the existence of the world is offered by the jokes that present the obvious as if it were a brand new piece of news. Wittgenstein writes: "This is certainly true, that the information 'That is a tree,' when no one could doubt it, might be a kind of *joke* and as such have meaning. A *joke* of this kind was in fact made once by Renan" (Wittgenstein, *Certainty*: 60e-61e [italics mine]). Freud introduces a certain number of self-evident jokes comparable to the "this is a tree" example of Wittgenstein and even, why not, to the "I know that I have two hands" example of Moore. Here is one of them: "How beautifully Nature has arranged it that as soon as a child comes into the world it finds a mother ready to take care of it!" (Freud, *Jokes*: 69). In these cases, the pleasure provided by the joke consists in treating a grammatical proposition *as if* it were an empirical proposition. But what about this "as if"? Is it not perhaps the core of innovative action? To bring the foundation of a certain linguistic game to the surface, hypothesizing for a moment its ability to assimilate the array of empirical facts, is the only way to move gradually on to a different game, one governed by a different set of rules.

Sophistical fallacies are no longer such when, and only when, what is in question is a change in that "basis" or "substratum" which allows us to discriminate between an appropriate and a fallacious move. Just as a grammatical proposition is *not* true (or false, naturally) so the paralogistic argumentative procedure that modifies the demarcation between what is grammatical and what is empirical is *not* false (or true, naturally). The same diagnosis that Wittgenstein formulates with regard to Moore's truisms is also appropriate for the *use* of sophistic fallacies in a crisis situation. Wherever the foundation of a linguistic game is concerned, it is *always* nonsensical to speak of correctness or incorrectness. It is nonsensical if this foundation holds as it should; but it is no less nonsensical if this foundation is subjected to conspicuous transformative traction. Wittgenstein writes: "If the true is what is grounded, then the ground is not true, not yet false" (Wittgenstein, *Certainty*: 28e). Productive fallacy, which distinguishes innovative action (and the joke), is not erroneous for the same reason that prevents us from considering the statement "I know that I have two hands" as true knowledge. Both paralogisms (based on the multiple usage of the same material) used by the Schumpeterian entrepreneurs and those (based instead on semantic transposition) that allow men and women to actualize a sociopolitical exodus, concur to alter the grammar of a form of life. Paraphrasing Wittgenstein, we could say: if false is false with regard to a foundation, paralogisms that support innovative action are never false (or erroneous or fallacious), since their employment aims at redefining a foundation as such.

b) What happens if the grammatical foundation, from which we derive the criteria for judging an act, fogs up, manifests a progressive instability and shatters? The "substratum of all my searching and of all my assertions" becomes then the object of much searching and of many assertions. Empirical propositions, which at one point had rigidified into rules, now return to the fluid state. Wittgenstein writes: "It might be imagined that some propositions, of the form of empirical propositions, were hardened and functioned as channels for such empirical propositions as were not hardened but fluid; and that this relation altered with time, in that fluid propositions hardened, and hard ones became fluid" (ibid: 15e). This is the phenomenology of crisis. Let us speculate now as to what its logic might be.

The relation between the grammatical and the empirical "changes with time." It can be supposed, however, that within the temporal arc in which change occurs, it becomes difficult—or nonsensical, or truly *fallacious*—to separate with clarity grammar from empiricism, *quaestio juris* from *quaestio facti*. As we have seen repeatedly, the two contexts are juxtaposed upon each other and then become hybrid. When "fluid propositions harden, and hard ones become fluid," we are left to unravel a number of *semihardened and semifluid propositions*. They reveal the contingent tenor of rules as well as the regulative capacity of contingent actions. Semihardened or semifluid propositions outline a context in which each *quaestio juris* is always also a *quaestio facti* and, vice versa, each *quaestio facti* is always also a *quaestio juris*. This intermediate state—let us say: the *regularity* or "common behavior of all mankind"—is the privileged terrain of innovative action (as well as being, obviously, the terrain of jokes). If, on one hand, innovative action provokes or accelerates the fluidification of old grammatical constructs, it fosters, on the other hand, the hardening of some empirical facts into a different normative "substratum" or "foundation." What is certain is that semihardened or semifluid propositions that surround the state of exception displace well-formed deductions and argumentations free of ambiguity. Otherwise put: the logic of crisis has its canon in syllogisms with three or more premises, in the switching of the consequent with its antecedent ("from grammatical to empirical" is legitimately reversed into the movement "from empirical to grammatical"), in amphiboly and homonymy, in the exchange between heterogeneous categories (halfway through my argument I begin treating the grammatical as empirical, or vice versa), in the attribution to the subject of the accidental properties of its predicate, and so on. The logic of crisis, in conclusion, has its authentic canon in irregular or "paralogistic" inferences.

At the exact point when a form of life cracks and self combusts, the question of *giving shape to life as such* is back on the agenda, even though it lies within a peculiar historical context. During the crisis, human praxis positions itself again near that threshold (an ontogenetic but also transcendental threshold) where verbal language hinges on nonlinguistic drives, reshaping them from top to bottom; it positions itself again, therefore, at the Archimedean point where screaming and pain are substituted by discourse, or by fear, desire, aggression (See Chapter Four). The logic of crisis is most evident in the articulation between instinctual apparatus and propositional structure, between drives and grammar. Each attempt at delineating a different normative "substratum," though it unravels within wholly contingent sociopolitical circumstances, retraces and compounds, on a reduced scale, the passage from life in general to linguistic life. Anomalous inferences are the precision instrument by virtue of which verbal thought, delineating a different normative "substratum," recalls, each time anew, this *anthropogenetic* passage (see Virno, *Quando il verbo*: 75–88). Their anomaly lies in the manner in which language preserves within itself, though transfigured to the point of being barely recognizable, the original nonlinguistic drive. It is impossible to modify a historically defined grammar without reproducing in effigy the exit from pregrammatical life, with the means made available only by well tempered discourse.

Again Wittgenstein: "The mythology may change back into a state of flux, the river-bed of thoughts may shift" (Wittgenstein, *Certainty*: 15e). While "I distinguish between the movement of the waters on the river-bed and the shift of the bed itself ... there is not a sharp division of the one from the other" (ibid: 15e). This inscrutability demands, if we wish to describe it with a touch of realism, argumentations that can otherwise combine the initial data or turn the axis of discourse towards elements that were previously not taken into account. Since the state of exception is characterized by a real ambivalence (the river-bed is also the movement of the waters, the movement of the waters is also river-bed), it would be extravagant, and also patently wrong, to see a mistake in the ambivalent inference. This inference alone truly shows itself to be perspicuous in the gray area in which "the same proposition may get treated at one time as something to test by experience, at another as a rule of testing" (ibid: 15e). The fallacy alone faithfully demonstrates the twofold character of this proposition, since it reveals *at the same time* both its fluid and hardened aspect, its statute of fact as well as its normative disposition. The paralogism employed for the purpose of an innovative action within a critical situation displays the "lack of sharpness ... of the boundary between rule and empirical proposition" (ibid: 41e); furthermore, this paralogism draws attention to the case in which "rule and empirical proposition merge into one another" (ibid: 39e). That the same proposition should be treated at one time as a proposition to test *and* as a rule of testing is a characteristic of jokes: "I would never sign up for a club that accepts the likes of me." If we laugh, we laugh because the grammatical water-bed is transformed before our very eyes into an empirical flow of water, and the flow into a water-bed; or because the rule, being also a fact, is wittily applied to itself.

c) Wittgenstein compares the grammar of a form of life to "the axis around which a body rotates" (ibid: 22e). This means that the authority of these rules depends entirely upon the congregate of their applications: "this axis is not fixed in the sense that anything holds it fast, but the movement around it determines its immobility" (ibid: 22e). The foundation that allows one to evaluate the moves in a linguistic game is nothing other, if you will, than an effect, or even the *residue* of these moves. The autonomy of the applicative moment, even its absolute priority, manifests itself again here (see Chapter Four). The grammatical proposition, far from directing linguistic praxis step by step, "only gets sense from the rest of our procedure of asserting" (ibid: 22e). This is exactly what Carl Schmitt says with regard to the realization of the juristic rule. Our "ulterior assertion" alone will decide the fate of the "background" or "substratum" upon which we judge empirical assertions as true or false.

Insisting on this backward movement of the empirical (application) on the grammatical (rule), Wittgenstein writes: "I have arrived at the rock bottom of my convictions. And one might almost say that these foundation-walls are carried by the whole house" (ibid: 33e). Now, if the walls are held up by the house that they themselves seem to hold up, we can suppose that these foundation-walls can be also modified, and even replaced, by means of a progressive remodeling of rooms, stairs, and rooftop. The movement around the rotational axis can guarantee the stability of this movement or radically discredit it. The application of the rule has the first and last word. "Certain events would put me into a position in which I could not go on with the old language-game any further. In which I was torn away from the *sureness* of the game. Indeed, doesn't it seem obvious that the possibility of a language-game is conditioned by certain facts?" (ibid: 82e [italics mine]). The events that interfere with continuing the "old language-game" are simply misleading and unusual applications of its rules. What is misleading and unusual is the applicative decision that replaces the disjunctive "or" with the paratactic "and" (as in the joke of the leaky kettle); or that does not accept affirmation and negation according to the same relationship; or that assumes in a compound sense that which the interlocutor has asserted in a divided sense; or that enhances the value of the semantic ambiguity of a certain sentence. The "given facts" that threaten the sureness of the language-game are single moves characterized by a *counterfactual*, or, in any case, *heuristic use* of argumentative fallacies. Having examined this use earlier (see Chapter Six) so as to avoid confusion and misunderstandings, this use now finds its appropriate place within the *theory of crisis* outlined by Wittgenstein (and stubbornly ignored by all of Wittgenstein's scholars). Our "ulterior assertion" dethrones the grammatical certainties upon which it is founded, utilizing paralogism as the premise of hypothetical reasoning. Jokes and innovative action displace the "rotational axis" of a form of life by means of an openly "fallacious" conjecture, one that nonetheless reveals in a flash a different way of applying the rules of the game: contrary to the way it seemed before, it is entirely possible to embark on a side path or to escape from Pharaoh's Egypt.

Epilogue

In no small number are those who equate jokes to the "Sunday of Life," or to a Mardi Gras hiatus when it is finally legitimate to transgress and mock the order that is in place during the normal work week. I am not at all fond of this point of view. Above all, because I see nothing as being more melancholy and prone to resignation than the desire to transgress. Furthermore, and this is what counts most, because this way of thinking obfuscates what really matters in jokes.

In this essay I have never emphasized the content of jokes (which is not always irreverent with regard to the establishment and to social hierarchies); rather, I have focused my attention on the *logicolinguistic resources* that jokes utilize. I have done so with the conviction that innovative action, in general, draws upon the same essential resources as jokes. As I said in the beginning of this essay, joke-making is a very specific language-game, one that shows, in filigree detail, that all language-games can be transformed. Jokes reveal a unique interweaving of the *operative* level and the *metaoperative* level of functioning. They reveal a particular operation whose distinguishing feature is the isolation of those traits common to the multiple operations that can shatter the state of equilibrium of praxis. Jokes, like geographical maps, present, in reduced scale, the techniques that allow us to modify a form of life. But they present them *while* using these techniques to achieve something unexpected. In this sense, jokes resemble a map centered around one point of the territory depicted by the map: the image of its totality, but also of its circumscribed focus.

Any analysis of *Witz* tries to emphasize constitutive ambivalence: much has been written about the coexistence of hidden meanings and manifest meanings, or about the simultaneous use of the figurative and literal meanings of a given word. There is nothing wrong with this. I have, however, attempted to point out the truly crucial ambivalences, those that force us to recognize in jokes the diagram of linguistic praxis confronted by the state of exception. Now, by way of concluding, I will limit myself to recalling once again two examples of this course of action.

First of all: in the process of applying a *rule*, the joke (just like *phrónesis*) climbs up upon the shoulders of the rule and adopts, as a system of reference, "the common behavior of mankind." The first ambivalence is therefore that which lies between the determined *rule* and the *regularity* of species-specific forms of conduct. Jokes oscillate incessantly from one pole to the other, and they avoid being caught with their hands inside one cookie jar alone.

Second: a joke takes hold of the empirical and pushes it to the level of being grammatical, and pushes the grammatical to the level of being empirical, thus showing the interchangeable nature of both dimensions. This further ambivalence, interconnected but not identical to the previous one, consists of treating a riverbed as though it were a stream, and a stream as though it were a riverbed. Jokes, being the equal of innovative action, depend completely upon *semisolid or semifluid propositions*. Innovative action, like jokes, has its own toolbox; that is to say, its own logical framework, consisting of paralogisms that make it possible to produce or to utilize propositions of this kind.

PART 3

MIRROR NEURONS, LINGUISTIC NEGATION, RECIPROCAL RECOGNITION

Translators' Note:

In Hypothesis 2 of this essay, and in the corollaries to this hypothesis, where Virno illustrates how the "linguistic animal is the species capable of not recognizing its own kind," we find in his words echoes of a poem that will be very familiar to the Italian reader: "Se questo è un uomo" ("If This is a Man"), by the Italian writer and survivor of the Holocaust, Primo Levi. In the statement of the hypothesis, Virno places in quotation marks the words that "signal" the poem: "Even the perceptive evidence that 'this is a man' loses its own irrefutability ..." The elaboration of his argument, in the corollaries, recalls elements of the poem that embody the process by which the Nazi officer can come to "consider the old Jewish man to be 'not human.'" Here is the poem in its entirety:

If This is a Man

You who live safe
In your warm houses,
You who find, returning in the evening,
Hot food and friendly faces:
    Consider if this is a man
    Who works in the mud
    Who does not know peace
    Who fights for a scrap of bread
    Who dies because of a yes or a no.
    Consider if this is a woman,
Without hair and without name
With no more strength to remember,
Her eyes empty and her womb cold
Like a frog in winter.
Meditate that this came about:
I commend these words to you.
Carve them in your hearts
At home, in the street,
Going to bed, rising:
Repeat them to your children,
    Or may your house fall apart,
    May illness impede you,
    May your children turn their faces from you.

— Primo Levi, *Survival in Auschwitz*, translated by
Stuart Woolf. New York: Collier Books, 1987.

Se questo è un uomo

Voi che vivete sicuri
Nelle vostre tiepide case,
Voi che trovate tornando a sera
Il cibo caldo e visi amici:
    Considerate se questo è un uomo
    Che lavora nel fango
    Che non conosce pace
    Che lotta per mezzo pane
    Che muore per un sí o un no.
    Considerate se questa P una donna,
Senza capelli e senza nome
Senza piú forza per ricordare
Vuoti gli occhi e freddo il grembo
Come una rana d'inverno.
Meditate che questo P stato:
Vi commando queste parole.
Scolpitele nel vostro cuore
Stando in casa andando per via,
Coricandovi alzandovi;
Ripetetele ai vostri figli.
    O vi si sfaccia la casa,
    La malattia vi impedisca,
    I vostri nati torcano il viso da voi.

—Primo Levi, *Se questo è un uomo*. Torino:
Einaudi, 1976.

Mirror Neurons, Linguistic Negation,

Reciprocal Recognition

In this essay I will share some of the notes I have edited in preparation for a much longer work on linguistic negation and will focus on three interrelated hypotheses. I am not going to discuss them to the full extent that they merit; I will only endeavor to propose a clear and distinct formulation of these hypotheses. The first is derived primarily from an important essay by Vittorio Gallese, "The Manifold Nature of Interpersonal Relations: The Quest for a Common Mechanism." The other two concern the role played by verbal language in determining the sociability of the human mind.

Hypothesis 1. The relation of a human animal to its own kind is assured by an original "intersubjectivity" that precedes the very constitution of the individual mind. The "we" exists even before we can speak of a self-conscious "I." Thinkers such as Aristotle, Lev Vygotsky, Donald W. Winnicott, and Gilbert Simondon have variously insisted on this basic correlation of members of the same species. Vittorio Gallese, one of the discoverers of mirror neurons, has reformulated this correlation in a particularly insightful way, connecting it to a cerebral mechanism. In order for us to know that another human being is suffering or rejoicing, is looking for food or shelter, is about to attack or kiss us, we do not need verbal language; even less useful is the baroque attributing of intentions to the minds of others. All that is required is the activation of a group of neurons situated in the ventral part of the inferior frontal lobe.

Hypothesis 2. Verbal language does not serve as a powerful loud-speaker for this preliminary sociability which, after all, is shared by *Homo sapiens* and other animal species. That is to say, we should not believe that verbal language amplifies and articulates, with an abundance of means, the empathy of members of the same species that is already guaranteed at the neural level. Propositional thought provokes, instead, a rift in that original *co-feeling* ("*co-sentire*," as Franco Lo Piparo calls it) to which we owe our immediate under-standing of the actions and emotions of other human beings. Propositional thought does not expand neurophysiological empathy in a linear manner; instead, it interferes with it and, at times, suspends it. Verbal language distinguishes itself from other communicative codes, as well as from cognitive prelinguistic performance, because it is able to *negate* any type of semantic con-tent. Even the perceptive evidence that "this is a man" loses its own irrefutability whenever it is subjected to the function of the word "not." Language inoculates negativity into the life of the species. It enables the failure of reciprocal recognition. The linguistic animal is the species capable of *not* recognizing its own kind.

Hypothesis 3. Language is the antidote to the poison that lan-guage itself pours into the innate sociability of the mind. Aside from being able to cancel out neural empathy, completely or partially, language can also remove this contradiction. The species-specific intersubjectivity of the human animal is specifically defined by this double possibility. The public sphere is the unstable result of a tearing-apart and a patching-up of this intersubjectivity. In other words, the public sphere is derived from a *negation of nega-tion*. If this disturbs the dialectic echo of the latter expression, I am sorry, but I do not know what to do about it. It goes without saying that the negation of negation does not restore a solid pre-linguistic empathy. The risk of nonrecognition is introduced once and for all into the sphere of social interaction.

Corollaries to Hypothesis 1. Vittorio Gallese writes: "About 10 years ago a class of premotor neurons was discovered in the macaque monkey brain that discharged not only when the monkey executes goal-related hand actions like grasping objects, but also when observing other individuals (monkeys or humans) executing similar actions. We called them 'mirror neurons'" (Gallese: 522). The region of the pre-motor ventral cortex of the monkey, within which mirror neurons carry out the simulation, is the region pre-disposed to program motor behavior, "not so much in discrete passages (strength and direction of future movement), as in abstract passages of the global relation between agency and the goals of action" (Napolitano: 62). The experiment has been successfully extended to the human species. The presence of mirror neurons was established also in the human brain: to be precise, the neurons are positioned in the ventral part of the inferior frontal lobe, consisting of two areas, 44 and 45, both of which belong to the Broca region. When we see someone carrying out a certain action, "the same neurons are activated in our brain as would be if we were to carry out personally the same action" (ibid: 62). This is the neuro-physiological basis that allows us to recognize immediately the emotive tonalities of members of the same species and to infer the aim of their actions.

Mirror neurons, according to Gallese, make up the biological foundation of the sociability of the human mind. I understand the grief of other human beings by imitating their behavior at the neural level, thanks to the onset of innervation in the same tear glands that belong to me. This automatic and inadvertent co-feeling is what Gallese calls "embodied simulation." The interactions of a bodily organism with the world are radically *public*, always shared by the other members of the species. Inter-subjectivity, by far, precedes the formation of individual subjects; it cannot be explained by means of cognitive models employed by individual subjects. In the course of our interpersonal relations, much of what we attribute to the activity of a presumed ability to formulate theories on the minds of others derives in reality from far less "mental" mechanisms. This ability is simply the result of the capacity to create a "we-centric" space, as Gallese explains, that is shared by others. The creation of this shared space is supposedly the result of the activity of embodied simulation, defined, in turn, in subpersonal terms, by the activity of mirror neurons that allow us to map out the same neural substratum of executed and observed actions, sensations and emotions personally experienced and observed in others.

The identification of a "we-centric space"—a space where the "we" does not equate with a plurality of a well defined "I," but des-ignates, instead, a *preindividual* or *subpersonal* context—is the philosophically crucial point of Gallese's reflection. The Soviet psychologist Vygotsky, and the English psychoanalyst Winnicott, have shed light on the same issue, though by means of other argu-ments and in different terminology. For Vygotsky, the individual mind, instead of being a definite point of arrival, is the result of a process of differentiation that takes place within an original sphere of sociability: "The real movement of the process of development of infant thought is carried *out* not from the individual to the socialized, *but* from the social to the individual" (Vygotsky: 60). For Winnicott, an intermediate area between the I and the not-I dominates early childhood (the area of so-called "transitional phe-nomena"): this area does not connect two fully formed entities; on the contrary, it enables their subsequent configuration as distinct polarities. This relation thus predates the correlated terms (Winni-cott: 1–8). The important fact (for Winnicott, as well as for Gallese) is that this undifferentiated threshold, or preliminary "we-centric space," is not merely an ontogenetic episode that we leave behind; rather, it is the permanent condition of social inter-action. As Gallese observes: "The shared intersubjective space in which we live from birth continues to constitute a substantial portion of our semantic space" (Gallese: 525). This is not the moment for dwelling upon the unexpected convergence of such different authors. We must consider this convergence, however, a precious symptom of an objective theoretical *necessity*.

Gallese's thesis is encapsulated in this statement: "the absence of a self-conscious subject does not preclude ... the constitution of a primitive '*self-other* space,' a *paradoxical form of intersubjectivity without subjects*" (ibid: 518 [italics mine]). This rather radical formulation breaks ranks with the notion of egocentric (or, rather, solipsistic) simulationism, according to which the human animal is prone to generalize for other minds that which it has learned on its own. The above quote from Gallese postulates a simulation that is operative long before individual minds are formed, minds capable of learning, projecting, etc. The true merit of this position is that it liquidates many superfluous conceptual entities: an authentic "Ockham's razor," the historian of philosophy would say. It is wholly incongruous to attribute to verbal language the immediate intraspecies empathy which mirror neurons realize even "without self-conscious subjects." When "we are exposed to the behaviours of others ... we seldom engage in *explicit and deliberate interpretative acts*"; that is to say, it is not necessary to translate sensorial information into "a series of *mental representations* that share, with language, the propositional format" (ibid: 520). But it is even more incongruous to evoke a sequence of postneural and prelinguistic ghost-concepts, located halfway between mirror neurons and verbal language, incapable of accounting for both a cerebral simulation and a proposition. Gallese's thesis restores to each its own: to neurophysiology that which is neurophysiological and to linguistics that which is linguistic. In so doing, this thesis makes life hard for illegitimate claimants. In order to explain social relations, it is absolutely unnecessary, for instance, to assume that each human animal possesses an implicit "theory of the mind"; that is to say, that each is capable of representing to itself the representations of others. "If, while sitting in a public house, I see someone reaching for a pint of ale, I will immediately realize that my neighbour is going to sip some ale from it. The point is: how do I do it? In order to interpret the behaviour of the person sitting beside me in the public house, I must translate his biological motions into a series of mental representations regarding his *desire* to drink beer, his *belief* about the fact that the glass sitting on the table is indeed full of beer, and his *intention* to bring it to the mouth in order to sip beer from it …. I think that the view heralded by classic cognitivism, according to which our capacity of understanding the intentions determining others' behaviour is *solely determined* by metarepresentations created by ascribing propositional attitudes to others, is biologically implausible" (ibid: 520).

Corollaries to Hypothesis 2. The functioning of mirror neurons connects human sociability to the sociability of other animal species. We still need to address where the line of demarcation between the former and the latter lies, and what specifically constitutes this line. Let us quote Gallese again: "As shown by an impressive amount of converging neuroscientific data, there is a *basic level* of our interpersonal interactions that does not make explicit use of propositional attitudes" (Gallese: 525). I agree. But what are the effects of the grafting of verbal language upon this "basic level"? Do propositional attitudes (believing, hypothesizing, presupposing, etc.) acquiesce and empower the simulation that has already been accomplished by neuron mirrors? Or do they, instead, disturb and limit the range of simulation? I lean decisively toward the second alternative. I have no doubts as to the existence of a "base level" of sociability: provided we anchor it exclusively within the realm of neurophysiology. It seems to me implausible, on the other hand, to embrace the other idea, that verbal thought is limited to an ornamental and refining function for the "we-centered space" as circumscribed in time by mirror neurons. I believe, rather, that language destructively counteracts upon this "space," tearing apart its original compactness. The species-specific sociability of the human mind is characterized by such retroaction. In other words: this sociability is certainly qualified by the interweaving, but also by the lasting tension, and by the partial bifurcation, of neural co-feeling and propositional thought.

Every naturalist thinker must acknowledge one given fact: the human animal is capable of *not* recognizing another human animal as being one of its own kind. The extreme cases, from cannibalism to Auschwitz, powerfully attest to this permanent possibility. This possibility manifests itself mostly in a restrained manner, inserting itself, in faint and allusive manifestations, into the cracks of quotidian communication. Situated at the limits of social interaction, the possibility of nonrecognition has repercussions also within its own core, permeating its own entire fabric.

What does it mean not to recognize one's own kind? An old Jewish man is dying of hunger and cries out in humiliation. The Nazi officer knows what his fellow human being is feeling, by virtue of "embodied simulation": "the same neural structures that are active during the experience of sensations and emotions are also active when the same sensations and emotions are to be detected in others" (ibid: 524). But the Nazi officer is capable of disconnecting, at least partially or provisionally, from the empathy that is produced by mirror neurons. For this reason, he succeeds in treating the old Jewish man as a nonhuman being. It is too easy to account for the neutralizing of intraspecies co-feelings on cultural, political, and historical grounds. The naturalist, who is always ready to point out the invariable traits of human nature, can not treacherously wear, when it is convenient, the clothes of the relativist hermeneuticist. No three-card monte here, please. It goes without saying that the politicocultural dimension, as distinguished by intrinsic variability, has enormous weight in the concrete existence of any human being: what really counts, however, is focusing on the biological basis of this dimension and on its variability. The Nazi officer is capable of not-recognizing the old Jewish man, due to an absolutely natural (thus innate and invariable) characteristic of the species *Homo sapiens*. He is capable of not-recognizing him because his sociability is not determined merely by mirror neurons, but also by verbal language. If those neurons "that are active during the experience of sensations and emotions are also active when the same sensations and emotions are to be detected in others" (ibid: 524), then propositional positions, on the other hand, authorize the bracketing off and cancellation of the primitive representation of "others as similar to us" (ibid: 517). This bracketing off of neural co-feeling is due to what is perhaps the most typical prerogative of verbal language: *negation*, the use of the "not," the many ways in which a speaker can confine a predicate or an entire statement to the sphere of falsehood, of error, of the nonexistent.

Negation is only a verbal function, provided we do not give way to metaphorical or simply heedless uses of the term (based upon which, even a fist, in its own way, would be a form of denial). By pointing to white, I am not negating black. I am negating it if, and only if, I *say* "not black." The distinguishing trait of linguistic negation (but this latter adjective, I repeat, is pleonastic) consists in reproposing, with a reversed algebraic sign, one and the same semantic content. The "not" is placed before a syntagm that continues to express the thing or the fact of which we speak with all of its consistency. The thing and the fact continue to be designated, and therefore *preserved* as signified, at the same time as they are (verbally) *suppressed*. Let us suppose that the SS officer thinks: "the tears of this old Jewish man are not human." His proposition preserves and suppresses, at the same time, the empathy produced by "embodied simulation." It preserves it, since we are dealing here with the tears of a member of the same species and not simply with some form of dampness or moisture coming from the eyes. It suppresses this empathy by removing from the tears of the old man that human character which was implicit in the immediate perception-designation of these tears as being the "tears-of-an-old-man." By virtue of this power alone, the power to abolish that which we admit, or, more specifically, to suppress-by-preserving, can linguistic negation destructively interfere with a "sub-personal" biological device such as neural co-feeling. Negation (strictly correlated to the true/false dyad and to the modality of the possible) certainly does not obstruct the activation of mirror neurons; but it renders the signification of these neurons as something ambiguous and reversible. The Nazi officer can consider the old Jewish man to be "not human," even if he fully understands the old man's emotions by means of simulatory identification. Verbal thought destabilizes intraspecies empathy: in this sense, it creates the condition needed for what Kant has called "radical evil."

Hypothesis 2 serves as a premise to a host of conceptual and empirical investigations. It offers, perhaps, the key for an unusual reading of one of the most prestigious texts ever written on the social mind: Chapter Four of Hegel's *Phenomenology of Spirit*, devoted indeed to "the truth of self-certainty." It is widely accepted that the pages of that chapter present a story with a happy ending, that they outline the way in which reciprocal recognition can, in the end, be accomplished after multiple dramatic obstacles have been overcome. I see this as a misunderstanding. If we simply leaf through Chapter Four without preconceptions (if anything, hiding Hegel's book behind the last work by Churchland, in order to avoid making a bad impression), we immediately realize that Hegel's Chapter Four accounts for the different ways in which reciprocal recognition among linguistic animals can *fail*. Hegel presents a rich catalogue of checkmates and shots in the dark: the aggression that wipes out all empathy and drags us toward general self-destruction; the unilateral acknowledgment of the master on the part of the servant; the gradual emancipation of the subjugated nonhuman being who, in turn, ceases to recognize as a human being the one who had previously not recognized him; and lastly, the sarcastic coronation of the entire trajectory, the "unhappy con-science" that internalizes the negativity inherent in social relations, until aporia and failure become a chronic way of life. One could also say: Hegel, by delineating this chain of visible failures, shows how the living being who thinks with words can weaken, and, at times, turn into a game of chance, the immediate intraspecies sympathy that is the task of mirror neurons. Even when the human animal immediately deciphers the emotions and goals of its own kind, thanks to a neurophysiological device, this human animal is still capable of *denying* that this person is a kin. The possibility of nonrecognition: here lies Hegel's contribution to a naturalistic (though not at all idyllic) recognition of the species-specific sociability of *Homo sapiens*.

Within the range of conceptual and empirical research to be developed on the basis of *Hypothesis 2*, the investigation of linguistic negation stands out significantly, as we well know. There are not many modern logicians who have openly studied this negation, thus avoiding the necessity of calling it a primitive operational sign. As far as the linguists are concerned, in addition to exploiting certain rhapsodic accounts by Benveniste, one ought to read carefully (or reread with attention) Culioli's essays on the various forms assumed by negation in historiconatural languages. The most promising literature on this subject, however, is available in the inquiries of experimental psychologists and in the writings of the metaphysical tradition. As far as the former group of inquiries is concerned, I will confine myself to recalling here the analyses of "relations among affirmations and negations" in infantile thought, analyses produced by Piaget and his collaborators. As to the latter group of writings, the fortress to be conquered is, and remains, Plato's *Sophist*.

It seems to me that the theoretical epicenter of Plato's dialogue, the concise discussion of how we can negate that which is, and affirm that which is not, describes meticulously an *ontogenetic milestone*. The transformation provoked in the early years of life by the grafting of verbal language upon previous forms of thought is examined in the dialogue in minute detail. The possibility of negating, of asserting what is false, of entertaining zealous relations with nonbeing, is not taken for granted; rather, it instigates a genuine experience of wonder and poses thorny questions: "...the saying of something that yet is not true—all these expressions have always been and still are deeply involved in perplexity. It is extremely hard, Theaetetus, to find correct terms in which one may say or think that falsehoods have a real existence, without being caught in contradiction by the mere utterance of such words" (Plato: 979). The *Sophist* is perhaps the only philosophical work that seriously contemplates the traumatic advent of the "not" in human life. In a certain sense, Plato's text speculates on what happens when a child, at a certain stage of development, becomes capable of telling his mother, in a fit of anger, "You are *not* my mother." The first and most decisive discovery of every novice interlocutor is the ability to say things as they are *not*: it is precisely this faculty that brings about a caesura with respect to prelinguistic drives, that allows for the violation, to a certain extent, of neural co-feeling.

The faithful portrait of an ontogenetic stage of development, as well as the claim to its lasting relevance, are not the sole motives for keeping an eye on the *Sophist* while we discuss the social mind—as naturalists, *of course*. There is more to be said. It is rather well known that for Plato, to negate a predicate means to assert that the object of discourse is "different" (*heteron*) with regard to the properties attributed to the object by that predicate. Heterogeneity has nothing to do with contrariety: "So, when it is asserted that a negative signifies a contrary, we shall not agree, but admit no more than this—that the prefix 'not' indicates something different from the words that follow, or rather from the things designated by the words pronounced after the negative" (ibid: 1004). When I say "not beautiful," I am not saying "ugly"; I am leaving the door open to a potential series of *different* predicates: "red," "boring," "kind," etc. These other predicates are not incompatible with the denied predicate, that is to say, with "beautiful": within a different enunciative context they can be correlated to the denied predicate. The *heteron*, which truly shows what is at stake in linguistic negation, helps us to understand the dynamics of nonrecognition among human animals. The Nazi lieutenant, who says "nonhuman" with reference to the old, weeping Jewish man, does non mean the *contrary* of "man" (he does not believe himself to be in the presence of a cat or a plant). He means something *different* from a "man": for example, "totally inert," "deprived of any dignity," "such as to express himself only with inarticulate laments." Nobody can state that the Jew (or the Arab, in the case of Oriana Fallaci) is the logical opposite of the predicate "human," since mirror-neurons attest to the membership to the same species of the living creature in question. Nonrecognition takes root, instead, in the linguistic power to evoke a *diversity* that, in itself potential and undetermined, is circumscribed in each instance by resorting to some contingent property (the factual behavior of the Jew or of the Arab, for instance). When a child tells his mother "You are *not* my mother," the child is actually saying that she is *not* what she undoubtedly *is*, from other angles of perception. The child is gaining familiarity with the *heteron*, with the "different." The Nazi and Oriana Fallaci exhibit the atrocious profile of this same familiarity.

Corollaries to Hypothesis 3. Language does not civilize aggression between species; rather it radicalizes it beyond measure, taking it to the extreme limit of the *non*recognition of one's own kin. It is certainly legitimate to state that propositional thought reshapes, from head to toe, neurophysiological co-feeling. Except for one essential specification: "to reshape" means, *above all*, that propositional thought eats away at the original certainty of co-feeling. This tragic erosion, in and of itself, opens the way to a complex and malleable socialization clustered together with promises, rules, pacts, and collective endeavors. It would be wrong to believe that a discourse intended to persuade interlocutors is the "cultural" extension of "natural" empathy, empathy instituted from the very beginning by mirror neurons. Persuasive discourse is not at all the *natural* answer to the laceration of neurophysiological empathy put into effect by linguistic negation. Rhetorical argumentation, with all of its expressive finesse, internalizes the possibility of nonrecognition and it foils it, time and again. It does nothing but deactivate, with perspicuous propositions, the partial deactivation of co-feeling provoked by propositional thought. In the 23rd and 25th paragraphs of his *Philosophical Investigations*, Wittgenstein states that the "natural history" of our species consists (also) of a host of linguistic practices: commanding, interrogating, narrating, chatting, elaborating hypotheses, making jokes, thanking, cursing, greeting, etc. So then, these linguistic practices keep in check the negativity inoculated into animal life through verbal language itself: they regulate the use of the "not" and limit the reach of the *heteron*; to summarize, they allow for reciprocal recognition among living beings who could otherwise *not*-recognize each other.

The typically human public sphere finds its center of gravity in a *negation of negation*: it is a "not" that is positioned at the front of the latent syntagm "not-human." The power of linguistic negation explicates itself also with regard to itself: the "not" that suppresses-and-preserves can itself be suppressed (and preserved, as a catastrophic eventuality, liable to infinite postponement). The "we-centered-space," unveiled by embodied simulation at the moment of birth, does not become a public sphere by way of evolutionary strengthening; quite the contrary: it does so as a consequence of its own process of debilitation, a process loaded with risks. The "we-centered-space" and the public sphere are the two ways, parallel yet incommensurable, in which the innate sociability of the mind manifests itself, *before* and *after* the experience of linguistic negation. Before this experience, there is a compact and infallible neural co-feeling; then comes the uncertainty of persuasion, the tumultuous metamorphoses of productive cooperation, the harshness of political conflicts. In order to define the negation of negation, thanks to which verbal language inhibits "radical evil" (which language itself has made possible), I want to make use of a theological-political concept with quite a troubled history: the concept of *katechon*. This term, used in the apostle Paul's Second Epistle to the Thessalonians, as we saw in the opening essay of this book, signifies specifically the "force that restrains." *Katechon* is the device that ceaselessly postpones total destruction: the end of the world for the theologian, the unraveling of the social order according to medieval and modern political thought. Verbal language is a naturalistic *katechon*, one that, by supporting the formation of a public sphere, *keeps at bay* the catastrophe of non-recognition. This is, however, a very particular type of *katechon*, since it safeguards the "radical evil" that it has engendered: the antidote, here, is no different from the poison.

Mirror neurons, linguistic negation, reciprocal recognition: these are the coexistent, and yet also contradictory, factors that configure the social mind of our species. Their dialectic undermines the foundation of any political theory (Chomsky's, for example) that postulates an original "creativity of language," a creativity that is then repressed and degraded by power structures that become more inequitable, the more *unnatural* they become. The fragility of the "we-centered space," due to the negativity ingrained in verbal language, must, instead, construct the realistic presupposition of every political movement that aims at a radical transformation of the present state of things. A great and frightful political philosopher, Carl Schmitt, has written with evident sarcasm: "The radicalism vis-à-vis state and government grows in proportion to the radical belief in the goodness of man's nature" (Schmitt, *Concept*: 61). The time has come to refute this statement. An adequate analysis of the social mind makes it possible for a "radicalism vis-à-vis state" (and vis-à-vis the capitalist mode of production) to be based on the dangerousness of human nature, rather than on its imaginary harmony. For political anticapitalist and antistate action there is no positive presupposition to be vindicated. Its eminent duty is to experiment with new and more effective ways of negating negation, of placing "not" in front of "not human." If it attains its goal, this action embodies a "force that restrains," a force called *katechon*.

Bibliography

Note: English translations from books and essays existing only in Italian are by the translators.

Arendt, Hannah. *Lectures on Kant's Political Philosophy*. Chicago: The University of Chicago Press, 1992.

Aristotle. *The Art of Rhetoric*, translated by H. C. Lawson-Tancred. London: Penguin Books, 2004.

Aristotle. *The Ethics of Aristotle*, translated by J. A. K. Thomson. London: Penguin Books, 1958.

Aristotle. *The Organon: The Categories; On Interpretation; Prior Analytics*, translated by Harold P. Cooke and Hugh Tredennick. Cambridge, Massachusetts: Harvard University Press, 1955.

Aristotle. *The Politics*, translated by T. A. Sinclair; revised by Trevor J. Saunders. London: Penguin Books, 1992.

Aristotle. *Posterior Analytics; Topica*, translated by E. S. Forster. Cambridge, Massachusetts: Harvard University Press, 2004.

Aristotle. *On Sophistical Refutations; On Coming-to-be and Passing-away; On the Cosmos*, translated by E. S. Forster and D. J. Furley. Cambridge, Massachusetts: Harvard University Press, 2000.

Benveniste, Émile. *Problèmes de linguistique générale II* (1974). *Problemi di linguistica generale II*, translated into Italian by Maria Vittoria Giuliani. Milano: Il Saggiatore: 1985.

Cellucci, Carlo. *Filosofia e matematica*. Roma: Laterza, 2002.

Culioli, Antoine. *Pour une linguistique de l'énonciation*. 3 vols. Paris: Seuil, 1985.

Chomsky, Noam. *Language and Problems of Knowledge*. Cambridge, Massachusetts: MIT Press, 1996.

De Carolis, Massimo. *Tempo di esodo: La dissonanza tra sistemi sociali e singolarità*. Roma: Manifestolibri, 1994.

De Carolis, Massimo. *La vita nell'epoca della sua riproducibilità tecnica*. Torino: Bollati Boringhieri, 2004.

Esposito, Roberto. *Immunitas*. Torino: Einaudi, 2001.

Freud, Sigmund. *Der Witz und seine Beziehung zum Unbewussten* (1905). *Jokes and Their Relation to the Unconscious*, translated by James Strachey. New York: W. W. Norton & Company, 1963.

Freud, Sigmund. *Das Unbehagen in der Kultur* (1929). *Civilization and Its Discontents*, translated by James Strachey. New York: W. W. Norton & Company, 1961.

Gallese, Vittorio. "The Manifold Nature of Interpersonal Relations: The Quest for a Common Mechanism" in *Philosophical Transactions of the Royal Society; B: Biological Sciences* (2003):
http://journals.royalsociety.org/content/uta2fm7w4y0w51yb/fulltext.pdf.

Garroni, Emilio. *Creatività* in *Enciclopedia Einaudi*, vol. IV. Torino: Einaudi, 1978.

Gehlen, Arnold. *Der Mensch: Seine Natur und seine Stellung in der Welt* (1940). *Man, His Nature and Place in the World*, translated by Clare McMillan and Karl Pillemer. New York: Columbia University Press, 1988.

Gehlen, Arnold. *Urmensch und Spätkultur: Philosophische Ergebnisse und Aussagen* (1956). *L'origine dell'uomo e la tarda cultura*, translated into Italian by Elisa Tetamo. Milano: Il Saggiatore, 1994.

Hegel, G. W. Friedrich. *Die Phänomenologie des Geistes* (1807). *Phenomenology of Spirit*, translated by A. V. Miller. Oxford: Oxford University Press: 1977.

Hobbes, Thomas. *De Cive* (1642). *On the Citizen,* translated by Richard Tuck and Michael Silverthorne. New York: Cambridge University Press, 2005.

Hobbes, Thomas. *Leviathan* (1651), edited by Richard Flathman and David Johnston. New York: W. W. Norton & Company, 1997.

Jakobson, Roman. *Signe zéro* in *AaVv, Mélanges de linguistique, offerts à Charles Bally.* Genève: George, 1939.

Kant, Immanuel. *Kritik der Urteilskraft* (1790). *The Critique of Judgement,* translated by James Creed Meredith. Cambridge, England: Cambridge University Press, 1952.

Kant, Immanuel. *Der Streit der Fakultäten* (1798). "The Contest of Faculties" in *Kant: Political Writings,* translated by H. B. Nisbet. Cambridge, England: Cambridge University Press, 1991.

Lo Piparo, Franco. *Aristotele e il linguaggio: Cosa fa di una lingua una lingua.* Roma: Laterza, 2003.

Lorenz, Konrad. Das sogenannte Böse: *Zur Naturgeschichte der Aggression* (1963). *On Aggression,* translated by Marjorie Kerr Wilson. London: Routledge, 2002.

Martino, Ernesto de. *La fine del mondo: Contributo all'analisi delle apocalissi culturali.* Torino: Einaudi, 1977.

Marx, Karl. *Grundrisse der politischen Ökonomie* (1939–1941). *Grundisse,* translated by Martin Nicolaus. London: Penguin Books, 1993.

Mezzadra, Sandro. *Diritto di fuga: Migrazioni, cittadinanza, globalizzazione.* Verona: Ombre Corte, 2001.

Napolitano, Francesco. *Lo specchio delle parole.* Torino: Bollati Boringhieri, 2002.
Piaget, Jean. *Recherches sur la contradiction,* 2 vols. (1973–74). *Experiments in Contra-diction,* translated by Derek Coltman. Chicago: University of Chicago Press, 1981.

Plato. *Sophist,* translated by F. M. Cornford in *The Collected Dialogues of Plato,* edited by Edith Hamilton and Huntington Cairns. Princeton, New Jersey : Princeton University Press, 1985.

Piazza, Francesca. *Il corpo della persuasione: L'entimema nella retorica greca*. Palermo: Novecento, 2000.

Saussure, Ferdinand de. *Écrits de linguistique générale* (2002). *Writings in General Linguistics*, translated by Carol Sanders and Matthew Pires. New York: Oxford University Press, 2006.

Schmitt, Carl. *Politische Theologie: Vier Kapitel zur Lehre der Souveränität* (1922). *Political Theology: Four Chapters on the Concept of Sovereignty*, translated by George Schwab. Chicago: University of Chicago Press, 2005.

Schmitt, Carl. *Der Begriff des Politischen* (1932). *The Concept of the Political*, translated by George Schwab. New Brunswick, New Jersey: Rutgers University Press, 1976.

Schmitt, Carl. *Über die drei Arten des rechtswissenschaftlichen Denkens* (1934). *On the Three Types of Juristic Thought*, translated by Joseph W. Bendersky. Westport, Connecticut: Praeger, 2004.

Schmitt, Carl. *Der Nomos der Erde im Volkerrecht des Jus Publicum Europeum* (1950). *The Nomos of the Earth in the International Law of the Jus Publicum Europeum*, translated by G. L. Ulmen. New York: Telos Press, 2006.

Schumpeter, Joseph A. *Theorie der wirtschaftlichen Entwicklung* (1911). *The Theory of Economic Development*, translated by Redvers Opie. Cambridge, Massachusetts: Harvard University Press, 1961.

Simondon, Gilbert. *L'individuation psychique et collective* (1989). *L'individuazione psicica e collettva*, Italian translation edited by Paolo Virno. Roma: DeriveApprodi, 2001.

Todorov, Tzvetan. "La rhétorique freudienne" in *Théories du symbole* (1977). *Theories of the Symbol*, translated by Catherine Porter. Ithaca: Cornell University Press, 1982.

Virno, Paolo. "Virtuosismo e rivoluzione: La teoria politica dell'esodo" in his *Mondanità: L'idea di "mondo" tra esperienza sensibile e sfera pubblica*. Roma: Manifestolibri, 1994.

Virno, Paolo. *Esercizi di Esodo: Linguaggio e azione politica*. Verona: Ombre Corte, 2002.

Virno, Paolo. *Quando il verbo si fa carne: Linguaggio e natura umana*. Torino: Bollati Boringhieri, 2003.

Virno, Paolo. "Neuroni mirror, negazione linguistica, reciproco riconoscimento" in *Forme di vita*: n. 3–4, pp. 198–206. Roma: DeriveApprodi, 2004.

Virno, Paolo. *Motto di spirito e azione innovativa: Per una logica del cambiamento*. Torino: Bollati Boringhieri, 2005.

Vygotsky, Lev. *Mislenie i rec'* (1934). *Thought and Language*, translated by Alex Kozulin. Cambridge, Massachusetts: MIT Press, 1986.

Winnicott, Donald W. *Playing and Reality*. New York: Routledge, 2006.

Waismann, Friedrich. *Wittgenstein und der Wiener Kreis* (1967). *Ludwig Wittgenstein and the Vienna Circle*, translated by Joachim Schulte and B. McGuinness. Oxford: Blackwell Publishing, 1979.

Wittgenstein, Ludwig. *Philosophische Untersuchungen* (1953). *Philosophical Investigations*, German text with English translation by G. E. M. Anscombe. Malden, Massachusetts: Blackwell Publishing, 2001.

Wittgenstein, Ludwig. "A Lecture on Ethics" (1965) in his *Lectures and Conversations on Aesthetics, Psychology and Religious Belief*, edited by Cyril Barrett. Berkeley: University of California Press, 1967.

Wittgenstein, Ludwig. *On Certainty* (1969). Translated by Denis Paul and G.E.M. Anscombe, edited by G. E. M. Anscombe and G. H. Von Wright. New York: Harper and Row, 1969.

SEMIOTEXT(E) Post-Political Politics

AUTONOMIA
Post-Political Politics
Edited by Sylvère Lotringer and Christian Marazzi

Semiotext(e) is reissuing in book form its legendary magazine issue Autonomia: Post-Political Politics, originally published in New York in 1980. Edited by Sylvère Lotringer and Christian Marazzi with the direct participation of the main leaders and theorists of the Autonomist movement (including Antonio Negri, Mario Tronti, Franco Piperno, Oreste Scalzone, Paolo Virno, Sergio Bologna, and Franco Berardi), this volume is the only first-hand document and contemporaneous analysis that exists of the most innovative post-'68 radical movement in the West.

7 x 10 • 340 pages • ISBN-13: 978-1-58435-053-8 • $24.95

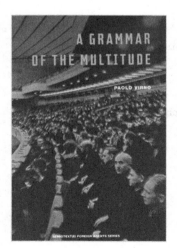

A GRAMMAR OF THE MULTITUDE
Paolo Virno, Translated by Isabella Bertoletti, James Cascaito and Andrea Casson

Globalization is forcing us to rethink some of the categories—such as "the people"—that traditionally have been associated with the now eroding state. Italian political thinker Paolo Virno argues that the category of "multitude," elaborated by Spinoza and for the most part left fallow since the seventeenth century, is a far better tool to analyze contemporary issues than the Hobbesian concept of "people," favored by classical political philosophy.

Drawing from philosophy of language, political economics, and ethics, Virno shows that being foreign, "not-feeling-at-home-anywhere," is a condition that forces the multitude to place its trust in the intellect. In conclusion, Virno suggests that the metamorphosis of the social systems in the West during the last twenty years is leading to a paradoxical "Communism of the Capital."

6 x 9 • 120 pages • ISBN-13: 978-1-58435-021-7 • $14.95

THE PORCELAIN WORKSHOP
For a New Grammar of Politics
Antonio Negri, Translated by Noura Wedell

In 2004 and 2005, Antonio Negri held ten workshops at the Collège International de Philosophie in Paris to formulate a new political grammar of the postmodern. Biopolitics, biopowers, control, the multitude, people, war, borders, dependency and interdependency, state, nation, the common, difference, resistance, subjective rights, revolution, freedom, democracy: these are just a few of the themes Negri addressed in these experimental laboratories.

Postmodernity, Negri suggests, can be described as a "porcelain workshop": a delicate and fragile construction that could be destroyed through one clumsy act. Looking across twentieth century history, Negri warns that our inability to anticipate future developments has already placed coming generations in serious jeopardy.

6 x 9 • 224 pages • ISBN-13: 978-1-58435-056-9 • $17.95

CAPITAL AND LANGUAGE
From the New Economy to the War Economy
Christian Marazzi, Translated by Gregory Conti
Introduction by Michael Hardt

Capital and Language focuses on the causes behind the international economic and financial depression of 2001, and on the primary instrument that the U.S. government has since been using to face them: war. Marazzi points to capitalism's fourth stage (after mercantilism, industrialism, and the postfordist culmination of the New Economy): the "War Economy" that is already upon us.

Marazzi offers a radical new understanding of the current international economic stage and crucial post-Marxist guidance for confronting capitalism in its newest form.

6 x 9 • 180 pages • ISBN-13: 978-1-58435-067-5 • $14.95

ALSO FROM SEMIOTEXT(E)

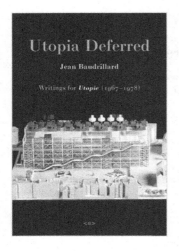

UTOPIA DEFERRED
Writings from *Utopie* (1967–1978)
Jean Baudrillard, Translated by Stuart Kendall

The Utopie group was born in 1966 at Henri Lefebvre's house in the Pyrenees. The eponymous journal edited by Hubert Tonka brought together sociologists Jean Baudrillard, René Lourau, and Catherine Cot, architects Jean Aubert, Jean-Paul Jungmann, Antoine Stinco, and landscape architect Isabelle Auricoste. Over the next decade, both in theory and in practice, the group articulated a radical ultraleftist critique of architecture, urbanism, and everyday life. *Utopia Deferred* collects all of the essays Jean Baudrillard published in *Utopie* as well as recent interview with the author.

6 x 9 • 328 pages • ISBN-13: 978-1-58435-033-0 • $17.95

THE CONSPIRACY OF ART
Manifestos, Texts, Interviews
Jean Baudrillard, Translated by Ames Hodges
Introduction by Sylvère Lotringer

In *The Conspiracy of Art*, Baudrillard questions the privilege attached to art by its practitioners. Art has lost all desire for illusion: feeding back endlessly into itself, it has turned its own vanishment into an art unto itself. Far from lamenting the "end of art," Baudrillard celebrates art's new function within the process of insider-trading. Spiraling from aesthetic nullity to commercial frenzy, art has become transaesthetic, like society as a whole.

Conceived and edited by life-long Baudrillard collaborator Sylvère Lotringer, The Conspiracy of Art presents Baudrillard's writings on art in a complicitous dance with politics, economics, and media.

6 x 9 • 232 pages • ISBN-13: 978-1-58435-028-6 • $14.95

FORGET FOUCAULT
Jean Baudrillard, Translated by Nicole Dufresne
Introduction by Sylvère Lotringer

In 1976, Jean Baudrillard sent this essay to the French magazine *Critique*, of which Michel Foucault was an editor. Foucault was asked to reply, but remained silent. *Oublier Foucault* (1977) made Baudrillard instantly infamous in France. It was a devastating revisitation of Foucault's recent *History of Sexuality* and of his entire œuvre. Also an attack on those philosophers, like Gilles Deleuze and Félix Guattari, who believed that 'desire' could be revolutionary. In Baudrillard's eyes, desire and power were exchangeable, so desire had no place in Foucault. There is no better introduction to Baudrillard's polemical approach to culture than these pages where he dares Foucault to meet the challenge of his own thought. First published in 1987 in America with a dialogue with Sylvère Lotringer: *Forget Baudrillard*, this new edition contains a new introduction by Lotringer revisiting the ideas and impact of this singular book.
6 x 9 • 128 pages • ISBN-13: 978-1-58435-041-5 • $14.95

FATAL STRATEGIES
Jean Baudrillard, Translated by Philippe Beitchman and W. G. J. Niesluchowski, Introduction by Dominic Pettman

In this shimmering manifesto against dialectics, Jean Baudrillard constructs a condemnatory ethics of the "false problem." One foot in social science, the other in speculation about the history of ideas, this text epitomizes the assault that Baudrillard has made on the history of Western philosophy. Posing such anti-questions as "Must we put information on a diet?" Baudrillard cuts across historical and contemporary space with profound observations on American corporations, arms build-up, hostage-taking, transgression, truth, and the fate of theory itself. Not only an important map of Baudrillard's continuing examination of evil, this essay is also a profound critique of 1980s American politics at the time when the author was beginning to have his incalculable effect on a generation of this country's artists and theorists.

6 x 9 • 232 pages • ISBN-13: 978-1-58435-061-3 • $14.95

Printed in the United States
by Baker & Taylor Publisher Services